Instructor's Manual and Test Bank

Step By Step
to College and Career Success

Third Edition

John N. Gardner

Distinguished Professor Emeritus, Library and Information Science Senior Fellow,
National Resource Center for the First-Year Experience and Students in Transition
University of South Carolina, Columbia

Executive Director, Policy Center of the First Year of College
Brevard, North Carolina

Betsy O. Barefoot

Codirector and Senior Scholar
Policy Center on the First Year of College
Brevard, North Carolina

Prepared by

Suzanne L. Hamid

Lee University

Bedford/St. Martin's   Boston ◆ New York

Manufactured in the United States of America.

4   3   2   1   0   9
f   e   d   c   b   a

For information, write: Bedford/St. Martin's, 75 Arlington Street, Boston, MA 02116 (617-399-4000)

ISBN–10: 0–312–68308–1
ISBN–13: 978–0–312–68308–5

Brief Contents

Contents

Introduction

Welcome to the Instructor's Manual and Test Bank for Gardner and Barefoot's *Step by Step to College and Career Success,* Third Edition. The contributors who assisted in writing this manual have drawn from their expertise and experience in the classroom. Here is what this rich resource has to offer:

Chapter Objectives

Objectives clarify the main points of each chapter and what is most important to communicate to first-year students in the teaching of that chapter.

Timing of Chapter Coverage

This gives an indication of when it is most useful to assign a chapter and suggests links to other relevant chapters that can be taught in conjunction.

About the Topics in This Chapter

Experts in their fields give suggestions on how to best present the material in each chapter.

Suggested Outline for Addressing Topics in the Chapter

The outlines offer a three-step plan for each session, weaving in items such as lecture launchers, chapter exercises, group activities, peer leader assistance, case studies, and more.

Test Questions

There are over twenty objective questions (true/false, short answer, multiple choice) that can be copied directly from this manual and used in the classroom. Answer keys are included. Each chapter also includes essay questions that can be used as the basis for writing activities.

Web Resources

Helpful Web links and additional resources complement each topic.

Additional Teaching Aids for Instructors

VideoCentral

VideoCentral is a growing collection of videos for the college success classroom. Hear from real students discussing their own experiences on transitioning to college life. Coming fall 2009.

Create a Book that Fits Your Students' Needs

Our Custom with Care program offers the highest quality books and media, created in consultation with publishing professionals committed to the discipline. Integrate your own material—such as specific school information or policies, academic calendars, or welcoming words to new students—or include only the parts of the text you intend to use in your course, or use any combination of these options. Visit **bedfordstmartins.com/custompub** for more information.

Get the Support You Need

Bedford/St. Martin's offers multiple training options to meet your needs, including workshops taught by several of our college success colleagues. Workshops will help you discover new ways to build rapport, communicate expectations, and monitor your students' academic performance. You will also have opportunities to share ideas with colleagues at other institutions, which will help you to create a dynamic and supportive learning environment in your first-year college course.

Integrating Technology in the Classroom

Web Links

Time Management Tips   www.gmu.edu/gmu/personal/time.html
George Mason University hosts this site, which gives instructions for taking a personal time survey as well as several useful ideas for better managing time.

Personal Goal Setting   www.time-management-guide.com/personal-goal-setting.html
This comprehensive site offers a wealth of information about personal goal setting and how students can turn those goals into action plans.

Learn to Prioritize   www.suite101.com/article.cfm/17943/103703
Ask your students to read this article, which explains how learning to prioritize can reduce the level of stress in their lives, academic or otherwise.

Printable Checklists   www.allfreeprintables.com/checklists/to-do-lists.shtml
Direct your students to this site, where they can print out free "to-do" lists. The site also offers free printable checklists for other activities such as grocery shopping and childproofing your home.

Procrastination Quiz   www.discoveryhealth.queendom.com/procrastination_short_access.html
This 15-minute online quiz identifies if your students are procrastinators, and if so, why and which areas of their lives are most affected.

Step by Step Central   www.bedfordstmartins.com/stepbystep
The free book companion site offers a variety of rich learning resources designed to enhance the student experience. These resources include video tips from real students; self-awareness exercises to assess your students' strengths and weaknesses; Quick Guides to refresh basic skills in grammar, writing, and reading; downloadable podcasts; and more.

About Freshman Seminars

Today, the Freshman Year Experience movement in the United States is nearly three decades old and well integrated into American higher education (Barefoot and Fidler, 1996; Cuseo, 1991; Sax, Astin, Korn, William, and Mahoney, 2001; Upcraft, Gardner, and Barefoot, 2004). While this movement has sought to stitch success into all aspects of university life and has promoted many interventions to enhance student success, freshman seminars by themselves have successfully addressed many of the needs of freshman students and have "tackled a long standing, seemingly endemic problem for higher education, the confusion and difficulties that cause many new students to drop out of college during or at the end of their freshman year" (El-Khawas, 2002).

In the 1980s, institutions of higher education became increasingly concerned about issues pointedly identified by Tinto (1975, 1987). Questions such as why do students leave college and what factors contribute to student success prompted colleges and universities to begin to implement a variety of strategies to enhance freshman success and retention. To this end, many institutions sought to create and boost fledgling first-year seminars in an attempt to improve student involvement and increase student retention (Upcraft and Gardner, 1989).

The freshman seminar is a course designed to enhance the academic and/or social integration of first-year college students into the institution (Barefoot and Fidler, 1996; Gordon, 1989). In the 2000 National Survey of First-Year Seminar Programming conducted by the National Resource Center for the First-Year Experience and Students in Transition, five variations of freshman seminars were identified: *extended orientation* seminars, *academic* seminars with common content, *academic* seminars with variable content across sections, *basic study skills* seminars, and *professional* seminars. *Extended orientation* seminars were the most frequent type of freshman seminars reported and are more commonly referred to as "freshman orientation, college survival, or student success courses" (Linder, 2002, p. 1). The most frequently mentioned topics addressed in such seminars were academic skills, time management, personal development and self-awareness, transition to college, and career exploration.

In their landmark work on the Freshman Year Experience, freshman success was defined by Upcraft and Gardner (1989) as making progress toward fulfilling educational and personal goals by: (1) developing academic and intellectual competence; (2) establishing and maintaining interpersonal relationships; (3) developing an identity; (4) deciding on a career and life-style; (5) maintaining personal health and wellness; and (6) developing an integrated philosophy of life. We find that nearly three decades later, freshman seminars continue to help students do that and more (Linder, 2002; Skipper, 2002). Of the responding institutions in the 2000 National Survey of First-Year Seminar Programming (*n* = 1,013), the majority of institutions had one or more of the following "research-based goals" for their freshman seminar:

- Enhancing academic skills

- Helping students transition to college and providing an orientation to campus resources

- Helping students improve their self-concept

The evidence is compelling that there is a positive correlation between participation in the freshman seminar and many desirable experiential outcomes for both students and faculty in the seminar and in other discipline-based classes. Some of these outcomes include higher rates of freshman-to-sophomore retention (especially for minority students), higher graduation rates, higher grade-point averages, more frequent out-of-class interaction with faculty, more involvement in campus organizations, more frequent use of helping services on campus, and greater faculty use of innovative teaching strategies.

References

Barefoot, B. O., and Fidler, P. P. (1996). *The 1994 national survey of freshman seminar programs* (Monograph No. 20). Columbia, SC: University of South Carolina, National Resource Center for the Freshman Year Experience and Students in Transition.

Cuseo, J. B. (1991). *The freshman orientation seminar: A research-based rationale for its value, delivery, and content* (Monograph No. 4). Columbia, SC: University of South Carolina, National Resource Center for the Freshman Year Experience.

El-Khawas, E. (2002). Reform movements. In *Higher education in the United States: An encyclopedia* (Vol. 2, pp. 512–516). Santa Barbara, CA: ABC-CLIO, Inc.

Gordon, V. P. (1989). Origins and purpose of the freshman seminar. In M. L. Upcraft and J. N. Gardner (Eds.), *The Freshman Year Experience* (pp. 25–39). San Francisco: Jossey-Bass.

Linder, C. (2002). *The 2002 national survey of first-year seminar programs: Continuing innovations in the collegiate curriculum* (Monograph No. 35, pp. 1–3). Columbia, SC: University of South Carolina.

Sax, L., Korn, A. W., and Mahoney, K. (2001). *The American freshman: National norms for Fall 2001,* 36th Annual Edition. Los Angeles: Higher Education Research Institute.

Sax, L. J., Lindholm, J. A., Astin, A. W., Korn, W. S., and Mahoney, K. M. (2001). *The American Freshman: National Norms for Fall 2001,* 36th Annual Edition. Los Angles. Higher Education Research Institute.

Skipper, T. L. (2002). *The 2000 national survey of first-year seminar programs: Continuing innovations in the collegiate curriculum.* (Monograph No. 35, pp. 11–76). Columbia, SC: University of South Carolina.

Tinto, V. (1975). Dropout from higher education: A theoretical synthesis of recent research. *Review of Educational Research, 45,* 89–125.

Tinto, V. (1987). *Leaving college: Rethinking the causes and cures of student attrition* (2nd ed.). Chicago: University of Chicago Press.

Upcraft, M. L., Gardner, J. N., and Associates. (1989). *The freshman year experience.* San Francisco: Jossey-Bass.

Upcraft, M. L., Gardner, J. N., and Barefoot, B. O. (2004). *Meeting challenges and building support: Creating campus climates for first-year student success.* San Francisco: Jossey-Bass.

Peer Leaders in the Freshman Seminar

Undoubtedly, this trend of using peer leaders in freshman seminars is growing, and institutions are recognizing that students deliver a variety of services and assistance to their fellow students. In 1994, 8.2 percent of colleges and universities surveyed were using peer leaders in first-year seminars (National Resource Center for the First-Year Experience and Students in Transition). A recent survey by the Policy Center on the First-Year of College (2000), found that 25 percent were doing so. Why use peer leaders? The research clearly demonstrates that colleges and universities shape students' development and the impact of the peer group on individual students is powerful (Astin, 1993; Chickering, 1969; Heath, 1968). Research on peer teaching indicates that both the peer learner and the peer teacher learn significantly from collaborative learning experiences and that peer teachers demonstrate deeper levels of understanding for the information they convey to their peers and attain a stronger grasp for the course content (Bargh and Schul, 1980; Benware and Deci, 1984; Whitman, 1988).

Based on survey data from 31,661 students at 61 institutions, the National Study of First-Year Seminar Learning Outcomes conducted by the Policy Center on the First-Year of College (Swing, 2001) found that the use of undergraduate teaching assistants in freshman seminars was correlated with higher scores assigned to learning outcomes and satisfaction than those of students who participated in freshman seminars that did not use peer leaders. Gordon (1989) has emphasized that freshman seminars use pedagogical methods that facilitate active learning, high levels of interaction, and critical thinking. One of the ways by which these pedagogical methods are realized is through the peer support group, such as student groups and networks. Peers promote student-to-student interaction and the use of peer leaders to help facilitate first-year seminar courses (Gardner, 1996; Gardner and Hamid; 2001; Gardner and Hunter, 1999; Hamid and Vanhook, 2001). Such students are seen as "an invaluable resource to the first-year seminar when trained and empowered as part of a teaching team" (Strommer, 1999, p. 51).

The use of peer leaders in first-year seminars also appears to have a positive impact on the retention of first-year students. According to Tinto (1987), one of the major reasons for students dropping out of college is failure to establish a social network. Peer leaders are being used to bridge that gap. The positive effects of collaborative learning on student retention is documented in Tinto's (1987) research with adult students, which revealed that the single most important predictor of students' persistence to graduation was whether they were members of a peer learning group. Freshman to sophomore retention rates at numerous institutions showed an increase in the rate of first-year to sophomore-year retention by more than 6 percent (Hamid, 2001).

Following an extensive review of the literature on teaching and learning research in higher education, McKeachie (1986) concluded, "The best answer to the question of what is the most effective method of teaching is that it depends on the goal, the student, the content, and the teachers. But the next best answer is 'students teaching other students'" (p. 63). In a similar vein, Gardner (1996) pronounced, "I have heard of freshman seminars literally coming and going from campuses . . . I have never heard of a freshman seminar that added the peer leader component and then subsequently dropped this feature of the course" (p. 2).

Given the findings that peers exert influence on each other, it is no wonder that the use of outstanding student role models as peer leaders is one of the hottest trends in the freshman seminar course development in U.S. higher education today (Gardner, 1996). Educators are recognizing and harnessing the tremendous potential value wrought by the use of students to facilitate learning and personal development. Indeed, it seems reasonable to conclude that students listen to their peers and learn a great deal, perhaps the most, from other students. Why not use peer leaders as co-teachers of your freshman seminar?

References

Astin, A. W. (1993). *What matters in college? Four critical years revisited.* San Francisco: Jossey-Bass.

Bargh, J. A., and Schul, Y. (1980). On the cognitive benefits of teaching. *Journal of Educational Psychology, 72,* 593–604.

Benware, C. A., and Deci, E. L. (1984). Quality of learning with an active versus passive motivational set. *American Educational Research Journal,* 21, 755–765.

Chickering, A. W. (1969). *Education and Identity.* San Francisco: Jossey-Bass.

Gardner, J. N., (1996). "Power to Peers." *Keystone Newsletter.* Belmont, CA: Wadsworth Publishing Company.

Gardner, J. N., and Hamid, S. L. (2001). *Summary and recommendations.* In S. L. Hamid (Ed.), *Peer Leadership: A primer on program essentials* (Monograph No 32, pp. 97–102). Columbia, SC: University of South Carolina, National Resource Center for the First-Year Experience and Students in Transition.

Gardner, J. N., and Hunter, M. S. (1999). *Outcomes and future directions of instructor training programs.* (Monograph No. 29, pp. 107–110). Columbia, SC: University of South Carolina, National Resource Center for the First-Year Experience and Students in Transition.

Gordon, V. P. (1989). Origins and purpose of the freshman seminar. In M. L. Upcraft and J. N. Gardner (Eds.), *The Freshman Year Experience* (pp. 25–39). San Francisco: Jossey-Bass.

Hamid, S. L., and VanHook, J. (2001). *First-year seminar peer leaders, programs and profiles.* (Monograph No 32). Columbia, SC: University of South Carolina, National Resource Center for the First-Year Experience and Students in Transition.

Heath, D. H. (1968). *Growing up in college.* San Francisco: Jossey-Bass.

McKeachie, W. J. (1986). *Teaching tips,* (8th ed.). Lexington, MA: D.C. Heath.

Strommer, D. W. (1999). *Teaching college students: Ten tips for success.* (Monograph No. 29, pp. 107–110). Columbia, SC: University of South Carolina, National Resource Center for the First-Year Experience and Students in Transition.

Swing, R. (2001). *First national study of first-year seminar learning outcomes,* 2001. Unpublished summary. Available: Policy Center on the First-Year of College, Brevard College, Brevard, NC.

Tinto, V. (1987). *Leaving college: Rethinking the causes and cures of student attrition* (2nd ed.). Chicago: University of Chicago Press.

Whitman, C. E. and Underwood, V. L. (1985). Learning strategies: The how of learning. In J.W. Segal, S. F. Chapman, and R. Glasser (Eds.), *Thinking and Learning Skills* (pp. 241–258). Hillsdale, NJ: Lawrence Erlbaum.

1 Beginning Your College Experience
Setting Off on the Right Foot

Chapter Objectives

1. To discuss the questions that are typically of concern to first-year students
2. To clarify the differences between high school and college
3. To discuss the issues and circumstances that commonly apply to returning students
4. To explore what advantages might result from a college education
5. To establish a process of setting goals and encourage students to set goals that will contribute to their persistence
6. To discuss how students can best connect with the instructors
7. To introduce what behaviors constitute academic dishonesty
8. To provide students with tips for managing their finances

Timing of Chapter Coverage

This chapter should be assigned and discussed at the beginning of the course. It is essentially an overview of both the text and the course itself.

About This Chapter

The purpose of this chapter is to help students establish a deliberate, rational plan to guide their academic and extracurricular life. In presenting strategies, the authors of the textbook base their recommendations on an understanding of the research about retention/persistence (in particular, the research of Alexander Astin, Vincent Tinto, and E. T. Pascarella). This research shows correlations between specific student behaviors and persistence through graduation. Although these are simply correlations (and not causal relationships), they do suggest ways to help students adopt positive behaviors that will increase their chances of completing a degree. The topics in this chapter of the book are intended to show students that they can beat these odds.

Take time at the beginning of the course to present these strategies as simple, positive steps to success. Addressing these strategies will offer students some positive ways to increase their chances of completing a degree. Many of the persistence factors are revisited later on in the book. Addressing the topic of **high school versus college** is one way to do this; it will emphasize to the students the major differences between high school and college and offer suggestions to help them make the adjustments to college life. When you present this material on high school versus college, encourage students to use the chapter as a guide to understanding the changes they should expect in their first year and to think more deeply about these issues; finally, at the end of the term, you can return to the discussion and ask students to reflect on how they actually have changed.

Students need to be reminded, even informed, of the "help" that is readily available to them on campus and that by utilizing these services, their success as students could be ensured. The section on **Where to**

Go for Help on Campus, is crucial information for new students and they should be reminded about the importance of finding help and utilizing campus resources.

One of the basic threads of the text is the importance of **goal setting**. In fact, student success is linked to this process from the book's beginning to its end. Students who establish a deliberate plan of action for themselves significantly increase their chances for success. Thus, it is important at the beginning of the term to take up goal setting, and the exercises in Chapter 1 are a good starting point. Because this is the beginning of the term and your class is not yet built into a group, the personal nature of the exercises may preclude an open discussion about personal goals. It is important, however, that the exercises be processed.

Suggested Outline for Addressing Topics in Chapter 1

Step 1   Begin with a lecture launcher or icebreaker activity

Step 2   Employ a variety of classroom activities

a. Use the PowerPoint presentation
b. Expand on key lesson themes
c. Involve students in a group activity
d. Involve peer leaders
e. Engage students in learning through case studies

Step 3   Review

a. Address common questions and concerns about the topic
b. Writing reflection
c. Prepare for next class

Expanded Lesson Plan

Step 1   Lecture Launchers and Icebreakers

- Since this is the first chapter/week of the term, a good introduction is to have students participate in a variation of the Name Game. In this exercise, students introduce themselves by adding an adjective in front of their name that begins with the same letter or sound ("I'm Awesome Amy," "I'm Cool Kristina"). The trick is that each subsequent student must begin by listing all of the other students who were introduced before (similar to the game, I'm Going On a Picnic). The instructor should be the first and last to participate. This aids in name recognition both for the students and the instructor.

- Another icebreaker that's helpful is to have students interview each other. One way to approach this is to have students line up across the back of the room by their birthdays, with January on one end and December on the other. Then ask them to pair with someone next to them (this almost always assures they will hook up with a stranger). Have them interview one another (name, hometown, major, future goals, and so on). Give them five minutes, and then ask students to introduce their partner to the rest of the class.

- Generate a class discussion about some of the changes students have had to make in order to adapt to university life.

- Plan a dialogue between you and a former student (or your peer leader) and discuss the background, qualities, and expectations of a good teacher and a good student.

Step 2   Classroom Activities

a.   *Use the PowerPoint presentation to complement your mini-lecture.*

b.   *Key Lesson Themes*

- Discuss the purpose for taking this course. Explain the **syllabus** and answer any questions students may have. The more your students understand the syllabus, the better they will understand the course. Introduce the required assignments and expectations for the semester. Introduce the course calendar, highlighting **due dates**. Make sure that the students understand *how* to read the course **calendar** if you have one. Highlight the components of each chapter in the book. This will help the students become familiar with the text and make it a user-friendly book.

- If your class is willing to open up, this might be a good time to have a **question-and-answer session** regarding their concerns on *Managing Your Finances and Controlling Your Debt*. You might have better luck if you invite the students to write their questions, fears, or concerns on an index card. Make sure you let them know that they are not required to identify themselves. Collect all of the cards and answer accordingly.

c.   *Group Activities*

- Generate a class discussion on *Connecting with Your Instructors and Finding a Mentor*. Ask students to get into small groups and create a plan for finding a mentor.

- Another option is to create permanent peer groups within the course. Assign students to different "teams," either randomly or with certain criteria in mind (i.e., consider factors such as gender or major to help divide the students into a diverse mix). Give the students time to get to know one another, either over an activity (such as the one listed above) or perhaps the interviewing icebreaker suggested earlier. Before you end the session, have each group choose a name for their team.

d.   *Peer Leader Assistance*

- Distribute index cards. Ask your students to share some information about themselves: telephone number, e-mail address, birthday, campus box number, and so on. Compile a list with the names, numbers, and addresses of the students and give a copy to each student. Do not forget to include your numbers. Use the e-mail addresses to create a list-serve and the numbers to give your students a phone call during their first week of college.

- Give a testimonial on your academic career at your university. Be sure to include the qualities/ingredients that helped to make you a successful student. Share with the class some of the changes you have had to make to adapt to university life. Describe the faculty at your university whom you considered to be your mentor. Conclude with the role that person has played in your success as a student and as an individual.

- As a follow-up to this initial session, consider giving each of your students a call during their first week of college. Find out if they have any questions about the course, the syllabus, or the text.

e. *Case Studies*

ALICIA

Alicia is going to school and working a full-time job. Her employer generally supports her decision to be in college, but Alicia thinks her boss is asking her to take on more responsibilities than her schedule allows. Alicia decides to arrange a meeting in which she hopes they can both talk frankly about the problem, but she worries that her boss will think she's being "a complainer."

Discussion Questions

1. What should Alicia do to prepare for her meeting with her boss?
2. List some possible ways that Alicia's boss might respond to the issues she plans to raise in their meeting. For example, her boss might be angry or resentful that Alicia is asking to have some of her responsibilities reassigned. How can Alicia "plead her case" without sounding like the "complainer" she fears she will be perceived as?
3. If Alicia's boss refuses to reduce her workload, what should Alicia do?

SARAH

It's Friday and Sarah just got a weekend extension on the history essay that was due today. Friday evening her boyfriend calls and says he wants to drive up and spend the weekend with her. She knows why he wants to come: It's because he's still nervous about their being in different cities. She doesn't think she can afford to socialize all weekend. She wonders if he understands how worried she is about her courses.

Discussion Questions

1. Should Sarah agree to the impromptu visit with her boyfriend?
2. What factors do you think led to Sarah's need for an extension in the first place?
3. How might Sarah better manage her time so that she can complete her assignments by the due date *and* still spend time with her boyfriend?

CARLOS

Carlos thinks his mother has some unrealistic expectations. She likes to tell him that the reason she never finished college was so she could work and give her children the chance to go. Now she expects Carlos to come through his first year with A's in all his courses. Carlos doesn't do all that well on his initial round of exams, and when his mother hears the results, she expresses her disappointment and lectures him about whether or not he's serious about the education she's paying for.

Discussion Questions

1. What are some possible reasons for Carlos's lackluster performance?
2. How do you think Carlos responded to his mother's lecture? How would you have responded?
3. What are some strategies for success that Carlos can employ to help improve his grades on future exams?

Step 3 Review

a. *Address Common Questions and Concerns of First-Year Students*

- *Why do I have to worry about setting goals? I like to go with the flow.*
  Answer: Setting goals is the first step toward achievement. It helps students to combat negative self-fulfilling prophecies and allows them to form positive ones.

- *Commitment issues? I had no trouble getting through high school!*
  Answer: Forty percent of all students who enroll in four-year schools never finish their degrees, but by applying certain learned strategies, students can set themselves up for success.

- *As a commuter, can I live at home and still be successful?*
  Answer: Commuter students should try to maximize their commuting time, either by reviewing notes (if taking public transportation), discussing issues (if commuting with a classmate), or even listening to taped lectures or notes they've recorded (especially useful for long car rides).

- *After being out of school for so many years, can I make it?*
  Answer: Of course you can make it. Sometimes returning students are the most diligent ones in the class. Of course they face special challenges.

- *Why do "they" want to change me? I like the way I am!*
  Answer: College will naturally change a person. Benefits of college include a lower divorce rate, a better appreciation of the arts, and greater self-esteem.

b. *Writing Reflection*

- At the start or at the end of class, assign your students a ten-minute freewrite. Let them know even before you give them the topic that this assignment will not be graded. Then pose a writing prompt—perhaps one on ensuring academic honesty. After the writing exercise, ask your students if any of them care to share what they've written.

Test Questions

Multiple Choice

Choose ONE answer per question.

1. College is different than high school because in college
   a. tests are given less frequently.
   b. you do more writing.
   c. in some courses you do original research.
   d. all of the above

2. In order to attain your goals, you should
   a. set specific goals.
   b. know why the goals matter.
   c. a and b
   d. none of the above

3. Research has found that students who involve themselves in class discussions
   a. don't take comprehensive notes.
   b. are teased by their peers.
   c. earn higher grades.
   d. don't remember much of what is discussed.

4. According to the text, academic freedom is
   a. not receiving a grade penalty if you irritate your teacher.
   b. the right of instructors to discuss controversial issues without losing their jobs.
   c. a and b
   d. none of the above

5. A mentor can be
   a. an academic advisor.
   b. an older student.
   c. a professor.
   d. all of the above

6. Plagiarism is
   a. cheating.
   b. a type of smoking.
   c. an illegal drug.
   d. none of the above

7. In identifying a possible mentor, look for someone who
   a. takes a special interest in you.
   b. encourages you to challenge yourself.
   c. offers to meet with you to discuss your work.
   d. all of the above

8. Which is NOT sound advice regarding financial aid?
   a. File for financial aid every other year.
   b. Ask for a reassessment.
   c. Meet all filing deadline dates.
   d. Inquire every year about *criteria-based aid.*

True/False

9. Fixed expenses are predetermined, recurring expenses, such as rent.

10. You should try to meet with your instructors one-on-one.

Short Answer

11. List five ways that college is different from high school.

12. Give three examples of the advantages of having a college education.

13. What's a simple way to help protect your credit card?

Essay

14. Identify and describe the strengths you possess that will be an asset to your completing your college education. Consider what might contribute to your risk of not finishing college and how you can best address potential obstacles.

15. Identify one staff or faculty person who cares about you and conduct an interview with that person.

Answer Key

1. d, p. 4
2. c, p. 5
3. c, p. 7
4. b, p. 7
5. d, p. 7

6. a, p. 8
7. d, p. 7
8. a, p. 11
9. true, p. 10
10. true, p. 6

Web Resources

Benefits of a College Education   www.ihep.com/Org.php?parm=Press/PR6.htm
You may direct your students to this 1998 press release, issued by the Institute for Higher Education Policy, announcing a report that "indicates that the benefits of a college education are more extensive and significant than generally recognized." There is a hyperlink to a PDF file of the actual report as well.

About Goal Setting   www.about-goal-setting.com/
This online tutorial takes roughly 20 minutes to complete; it showcases the "science of goal-setting" and how to apply it to your life.

Study Distraction Analysis   www.ucc.vt.edu/stdysk/studydis.html

Tips for international students   www.dartmouth.edu/admin/acskills/intl.html

Goal-setting for academic success   www.siue.edu/SPIN/activity.html

For More Information

Bronson, P. (2002). *What should I do with my life? The true story of people who answered the ultimate question.* New York: Random House.

Chopra, D. (1994). *The seven spiritual laws of success: A practical guide to the fulfillment of your dreams.* San Rafael, CA: Publishers Group West.

Combs, P. and Canfield, J. (2003). *Major in success: Make college easier, fire up your dreams, and get a very cool job* (4th ed). Berkeley, CA: Ten Speed Press.

Covey, S. R. (1989). *The seven habits of highly effective people: Restoring the character ethic.* New York: Simon and Schuster.

Staley, C. C. (1998). *Teaching college success: The complete resource guide.* Belmont, CA: Wadsworth.

2 Managing Time and Staying Motivated
The Starting Line for Academic Success

Chapter Objectives:

1. To help students get control of their time and their lives
2. To explain how using goals and objectives can guide planning
3. To establish the importance of setting priorities
4. To illustrate how students can avoid distractions and combat procrastination
5. To demonstrate how students can use a daily planner and other tools
6. To discuss with students how to organize their days, weeks, and academic terms
7. To explain the value of a "to-do" list
8. To discuss with students how to avoid overextending themselves and giving into distractions
9. To illustrate how time management relates to courtesy and respect in the classroom and on campus

Timing of Chapter Coverage

It is critical that students actively engage in organizing their time from the outset of the academic term. Although some students may not appreciate the importance of developing skills in time management — at least until they experience a sense of losing control over their time — it is important to link early information about time management to some of the differences between high school and college. For students who tend to ignore time management techniques, assigning tasks that require them to plan will assist them in the long run. Procrastinators will get a better idea of why they behave as they do when they explore learning styles and personality types later in the text.

About This Chapter

Students often do not want to "waste" time on planning and managing their time. They may think that these activities take more time than they are worth. They may also resist exercises that they perceive to be "busy work." One way to motivate students and to involve them in the activities in this chapter is to focus on time management as a life skill rather than as a study skill. For those who did not get into the habit of maintaining a planner in high school and do not necessarily intend to do so now, discuss how professionals use these tools in the world of work. Focus on how organizing one's time can assist in reducing stress. Today's students find more usefulness in maintaining a planner than in filling out a schedule form.

Whereas good time managers usually know they are good at managing their time, poor time managers may not be aware of how and when they waste time. This is especially true for students who were able to survive in high school without devoting a lot of time to schoolwork or without developing organizational strategies. Asking students to assess their attitudes toward time before they actually begin to keep a record of how they spend their time sensitizes them to their individual strengths and weaknesses. Other than making some general observations about the chapter, discuss and explain the time management system outlined in the chapter and use class time to process many of the exercises. **Note:** If you are using peer leaders to co-teach this course, let these peers take the lead when presenting this topic.

Suggested Outline for Addressing Topics in Chapter 2

Step 1   Begin with a lecture launcher or icebreaker activity

Step 2   Employ a variety of classroom activities
   a. Use PowerPoint presentation
   b. Expand on key lesson themes
   c. Involve students in a group activity
   d. Involve peer leaders
   e. Engage students in learning through case studies

Step 3   Review
   a. Address common questions and concerns about the topic
   b. Writing reflection
   c. Prepare for next class

Expanded Lesson Plan

Step 1   Lecture Launchers and Icebreakers
   - Ask students to complete the *How Do You Measure Up?* exercise on page 15. Encourage them to share their results and generate a class discussion on the responses that you get.
   - It's not inconceivable that some students will spend more time on e-mail, instant messaging, and general Internet surfing than they do on their studies. After generating a discussion on how much of their time your students are using on online pursuits, you can segue into a dialogue about daily planning (i.e., building more structured Internet time into their schedule) or even procrastination (i.e., making sure that Internet time doesn't become a time-sucking distraction from their school work).
   - When discussing time management principles, the phrase "work smarter, not harder" is often tossed around. But what does that mean, exactly? In the text there is a blank Weekly Timetable chart that students were asked to complete as homework. Have them trade charts with a partner. After the students have examined each other's schedules, ask them to create a more time-effective plan for their partner. Then ask students to share what they've learned from the assignment. Hopefully, this will illustrate the principle of working smarter.

Step 2   Classroom Activities

a. Use the PowerPoint presentations to complement your mini-lecture.

b. Key Lesson Themes

GOAL SETTING

Use Exercise *Try It!* on page 16 to lead a discussion on goal setting. This general exercise asks students to name three goals they would like to set for themselves over the next decade. Next, they are asked to list two measurable objectives for achieving those goals. Using this exercise helps reiterate what students have learned in Chapter 1, as well as impress upon them the importance of managing their time if they are to achieve their stated goals.

TIME MANAGEMENT AND CIVILITY

This may be an appropriate time to discuss having a code of classroom etiquette in order to ensure civility, tolerance, and mutual respect within all academic settings. Introduce students to a university community creed or covenant if you have one. If not, provide an example of one. It is important early in the term for students to understand differences in expectations between high school and college. It is important that as students plan their time, they acknowledge that they bear more responsibility for their own learning in college than they did in high school.

c. Group Activities

- Assign students into small groups of three or four. Within each group, assign roles. One will play the role of a student trying to study. The others should provide potential distractions such as a roommate who wants to chat, a floormate who stops by and invites the student out for a pizza, or a phone call from an old friend. As a group, these students should work together to create a skit illustrating how the beleaguered students could gracefully (but firmly!) remove themselves from potentially distracting situations. Have each group perform their skits for the entire class. Then ask the class to critique each group's skits.

- An alternative to this is to have students perform their skits impromptu (improvise as soon as the roles are assigned). Emphasize that those playing the role of the distracter need to be persistent, as this will test the student's ability to say "no."

d. Peer Leader Assistance

- Using their syllabi from all of the courses they are taking this semester, have the students schedule their exams and assignment due dates in their personal student planner. This will be a nice resource for them to keep since it will allow them to see what papers and tests they have during any given week for the entire semester. You may give extra points for this.

- Be prepared to discuss how you make time for different things in your own life, including setting time aside to study. Give a testimonial on how good time management is a major reason for your success as a student.

- Show the students your method of time management (planner, daily schedule) and explain how these methods have been beneficial to you.

- Share with the class your strategies for coping when "the going gets tough." Be honest; explain how some stress-related situations could have been avoided. This would be a good time to remind students about the numerous support services that are available on campus.

e.   *Case Studies*

TINA

Tina turns in her sample daily planner. It is filled in completely from 6:00 A.M. to 1:30 or 2:00 A.M. every day. As you read through it, you realize that this schedule is not an exaggeration. Tina commutes 75 minutes each way to attend classes. She is a single mother; her son and daughter are both in elementary school and are active in athletics, scout, and church activities. Tina works full-time to support her family and pay for school. She is taking 15 credit hours, including a laboratory science. Tina says she is so stressed out she is afraid she will never make it to final exams.

Discussion Questions

1.   How might you respond to Tina's concern that she will "never make it to final exams"?
2.   What are some of the things that Tina can do to keep from feeling overwhelmed?
3.   Are there any campus resources Tina can use to help ease her load?

CHARLIE

Charlie has always been a C student. Before coming to college, however, he decided that he was going to work harder and reach for higher grades. At first, his mission was successful. He studied mainly in the library, on a regular schedule, and used his planner to chart out and prioritize his "to-do" list. Before long, Charlie was making A's and B's. But at a Halloween party, Charlie met Vanessa. The two hit it off and before long were practically inseparable. Charlie saw his grades decline. He knew he needed to get his studying back on track, but whenever he blocked off study time, Vanessa would either suggest that they study together (in which case, Charlie accomplished much less than when he studied alone) or go off and pout. Charlie wasn't sure what to do. He really liked Vanessa and didn't want to lose her, but he also didn't want to have to sacrifice his GPA for a girlfriend.

Discussion Questions

1.   What are some things Charlie could say to Vanessa to help her understand his situation?
2.   How should Charlie handle Vanessa's pouting and suggestions that they study together instead of alone?
3.   Should Charlie break up with Vanessa?

Step 3 Review

a. *Address Common Questions and Concerns of First-Year Students*

- *Why should I keep a written list of the things I need to do? I can remember everything in my head.*

  Answer: By creating a "to-do" list, your students can prioritize the tasks they need to accomplish. They can also create a system of differentiating between academic assignments and personal errands, such as denoting each type with a different color. And of course, every time they complete a task, they are rewarded with the satisfaction of being able to physically cross it off the list.

- *I know I am a procrastinator. Why should I do things any differently in college than I did in high school? I work best under pressure.*

  Answer: As the text explains, recent research indicates that procrastinators are more likely to develop unhealthy habits like higher alcohol consumption, smoking, insomnia, poor diet, and lack of exercise. Procrastination can also seep into other areas of a student's life, creating a pattern of avoidance. It is best to get these tendencies under control earlier rather than later, or else the student could begin to feel overwhelmed by their commitments.

- *How can I manage my time when my roommate is completely disorganized and keeps me up all night?*

  Answer: Encourage your students to create a plan for their living space. They could work with their roommate to set "quiet hours" for studying or sleeping. If the student is not on good terms with his/her roommate, or the roommate refuses to comply, the student could approach the resident assistant or hall director to help intervene. As a last resort, the student could apply for a room reassignment.

- *How am I supposed to find enough time to study when I have to work to pay my way through school (or play a collegiate sport, or create time for my family)?*

  Answer: Impress upon your students that time management is key to juggling multiple commitments. Studying doesn't mean that they have to give up all non-academic pursuits. On the contrary, students who work or participate in sports often achieve higher grades than their less-active counterparts due in part to the important role that time management plays in their lives. However, if your student is truly overloaded with commitments and cannot reduce their load of responsibility, it may be time for that student to reassess whether or not right now is the time for their education.

b. *Writing Reflection*

Direct your students to pages 24–25 and ask them to do the portfolio exercise.

Test Questions

Multiple Choice

Choose ONE answer per question.

1. For each hour spent in class, you should schedule _____ hour(s) of study time.
   a. ½   c. 1½
   b. 1   d. 2

2. Two of the most cited differences between high school and college are increased autonomy and
   a. increased interdependence.   c. less responsibility.
   b. greater responsibility.   d. none of the above

3. The text recommends dividing study time into _____ blocks.
   a. 30-minute   c. 50-minute
   b. 45-minute   d. 60-minute

4. What is the most important reason to be on time for class?
   a. It shows respect for both your professor and your classmates.
   b. It affects your class participation grade.
   c. Your parents are paying for it.
   d. You might miss something you need to know for a test.

5. Procrastination is a _____
   a. learning style.   c. psychological disorder.
   b. trend.   d. none of the above

6. Block-scheduling literally means
   a. back-to-back classes.   c. classes once per week.
   b. 2-hr classes.   d. none of the above

7. Time management is
   a. unattainable.
   b. a lifelong skill.
   c. only achieved by Type A students.
   d. none of the above

True/False

8. The text recommends scheduling at least three aerobic workouts per week.

9. Maintaining a "to-do" list can help you avoid feeling stressed out.

Short Answer

10. Name three components of good time management.

11. Name one benefit and one drawback to block scheduling.

12. List three ways to avoid distractions while studying.

13. Name one thing you can do to demonstrate basic politeness in the classroom.

Essay

14. What behaviors do you consider to be rude and disrespectful? What role can you play in enhancing civility in the classroom?

15. Describe the top five ways that you organize your day. What are the strengths and challenges of these methods/ways/behaviors?

16. Which principle of time management do you consider to be the most important? Why?

17. What is your ideal class schedule and why?

18. Which principle of time management is your least favorite? Why?

Answer Key

1. d, p. 19
2. b, p. 16
3. c, p. 20
4. a, p. 22
5. d, p. 17

6. a, p. 21
7. b, p. 22
8. true, p. 19
9. true, p. 18

Web Resources

Time Management Tips   www.gmu.edu/gmu/personal/time.html
George Mason University hosts this site, which gives instructions for taking a personal time survey as well as several useful ideas for better managing time.

Personal Goal Setting   www.time-management-guide.com/personal-goal-setting.html
This comprehensive site offers a wealth of information about personal goal setting and how students can turn those goals into action plans.

Learn to Prioritize   www.suite101.com/article.cfm/17943/103703
Ask your students to read this article, which explains how learning to prioritize can reduce the level of stress in their lives, academic or otherwise.

Printable Checklists   www.allfreeprintables.com/checklists/to-do-lists.shtml
Direct your students to this site, where they can print out free "to-do" lists. The site also offers free, printable checklists for other activities such as grocery shopping and childproofing your home.

Student Organizer   www.primasoft.com/so.htm
Some students may benefit from an electronic organizer but cannot afford a PDA. In this case, direct them to the above link for PrimaSoft's Course Book software, which organizes everything from assignments to your own custom dictionary of terms. After a 30-day free trial, students who like the software may purchase it for a nominal fee.

Mastering Time 101   members.aol.com/rslts/101Frames.html
This free, online seminar presents less conventional methods of time management, focusing on rethinking the concept of time.

Techniques to manage procrastination   www.ucc.vt.edu/stdysk/procrast.html

Hints for planning study time   www.coun.uvic.ca/learn/program/hndouts/plan_ho.html

Mind tools for getting the most out of your time — index of articles   www.mindtools.com/page5.html

Control of the environment   www.ucc.vt.edu/stdysk/control.html

For More Information

Davidson, J. (2001). *The complete idiot's guide to time management* (3rd ed). New York: Alpha Books.
DeGraaf, J. (Ed.) (2003). *Take back your time: Fighting overwork and time poverty in America.* San Francisco: Berrett-Koehler Publishers, Inc.

Lagatree, K. (1999). *Checklists for life: 101 lists to help you get organized, save time, and unclutter your life.* New York: Random House Reference.

Merrill, A. R. and Merrill, R. (2003). *Life matters: Creating a dynamic balance of work, family, time, and money.* New York: McGraw Hill.

Sapadin, L. (1999). *Beat procrastination and make the grade: The six styles of procrastination and how students can overcome them.* New York: Penguin.

3 Thinking Critically

Searching Beyond Right and Wrong

Chapter Objectives:

1. To define and illustrate what critical thinking is and explain why there are no right nor wrong answers to many important questions
2. To discuss why critical thinking is an important lifelong skill
3. To identify and explain four aspects of critical thinking
4. To demonstrate how you can avoid faulty reasoning
5. To explain how college encourages critical thinking
6. To show why it is important to critically evaluate information on the Internet

Timing of Chapter Coverage

We recommend that you spend time early in the term helping students understand the differences between high school and college thinking. Some first-year students already may have been exposed to such a process, but it's still worth emphasizing; much of what college success depends on is the ability to work through ideas as opposed to memorizing a series of facts. If we want college graduates to be effective and experienced critical thinkers, the habit of critical thinking needs to be established early in the college experience so that it can be repeatedly practiced, refined, and developed throughout the remaining college years. The first-year seminar can help students develop critical thinking from the very beginning of college. Give students permission to voice their most absurd ideas without fear of criticism. Show how any idea must first be weighed against evidence before it is discarded. Stress the relationship of critical thinking not only to writing and speaking, but to most things that crop up in their daily lives: choosing what to do on a weekend, deciding on a field of study, planning a vacation, or repairing a car.

About This Chapter

Critical thinking involves reflecting on the information received moving from "surface" learning toward "deep" learning, and from learning by "transmission" of knowledge by the teacher or text to learning by "transformation" of knowledge by the learner. When students think critically, they not only know the facts, but they go beyond the facts and think about them in a different way other than how those facts have been presented in class or in the text. The following information can help you introduce your students to the practice of critical thinking, making sure they have a strong grasp on it as a concept before plunging into the text. The instructional strategies may be used to teach a particular course unit on critical thinking, or they may be used throughout the semester across different course topics.

**EXPLICITLY DEFINE CRITICAL THINKING FOR STUDENTS IN TERMS OF
SPECIFIC ACTIONS AND ATTITUDES THAT CAN BE PUT INTO PRACTICE.**

Students can use this list to determine whether they are actually engaging in critical thinking:

- **Application:** To apply theoretical principles or abstract concepts to practical, real-life situations and concrete problems (e.g., applying learned principles of critical thinking to class discussions and course exams).

- **Analysis:** To break down (deconstruct) information into its parts in order to see the relationships among these parts or the relationship between the parts and the whole (e.g., to identify the root causes of disagreements during class discussions; to distinguish relevant from irrelevant information; to identify and disclose hidden assumptions or biases).

- **Synthesis:** To build up (reconstruct), combine, or integrate separate pieces of information to create a new pattern or alternative structure (e.g., to combine related ideas discussed in separate sections of the course to form a single, unified product such as a written paper or concept map).

- **Evaluation:** To judge the truth or value of ideas, data, or products (e.g., to judge the quality of a logical argument using established standards or learned criteria for critical thinking).

- **Deduction:** To draw specific conclusions about particular examples that are logically consistent with or necessarily follow from general principles and premises (e.g., to deduce what particular enforcement practices or disciplinary actions would follow if the college were to adopt a general "zero tolerance" drug policy on campus).

- **Induction:** To draw out well-reasoned generalizations or principles from specific examples (e.g., to identify recurrent themes or categories among a variety of ideas generated during a group discussion).

- **Adduction:** To make a case for an argument or position by accumulating supporting evidence in the form of logical arguments, factual information, or empirical research.

- **Refutation:** To make a case against an argument or position by accumulating contradictory evidence in the form of logical arguments, factual information, or empirical research.

- **Extrapolation:** To extend, expand, or project beyond information given and identify its implications for other areas (e.g., to extrapolate from present trends to construct an image of the future).

- **Hypothetical Reasoning:** To create tentative ideas or explanations for purposes of testing their validity or predicting their accuracy (e.g., to develop a survey or questionnaire designed to test the hypothesis that students are dissatisfied with the social climate on campus).

- **Perspective-Taking:** To view an issue from different viewpoints or positions in order to gain a more complete understanding (e.g., to view an issue from the perspective of someone different than yourself in terms of gender, age, or race).

- **Divergent Thinking:** Wide-focus thinking that serves to generate many different ideas (e.g., brainstorming multiple potential solutions to a problem).

- **Convergent Thinking:** Focused thinking that eliminates multiple ideas to decide on one particular option or alternative (e.g., to identify the best solution to a problem from a list of different solution strategies).

INCORPORATE COMPARISON-AND-CONTRAST QUESTIONS INTO LECTURES, TESTS, AND ASSIGNMENTS.

During class discussions, raise questions that call for multiple student perspectives. (For example, "Who doesn't agree with what's being said?" "Would someone else like to express an opposing viewpoint?") Try the following strategies to engage your students in critically thinking about viewpoints different from their own:

- Use student-centered instructional methods that take you "off stage," exposing students to the perspectives of other students and reducing their perception of you as the absolute authority. For example, have students who hold diverse viewpoints on a certain issue join together to form (a) small discussion groups, (b) student debate teams, or (c) panel discussions.

- Play the role of "devil's advocate," using the Socratic method to prod students to see the pros and cons of their position on an issue. For example, persuade students to buy into a certain position, then proceed to expose its flaws.

- Have students engage in "reverse thinking" by requiring them to switch their original position on an issue being discussed in class. This can serve to combat "either-or"/"black-and-white" thinking and help students adopt a more balanced position on controversial issues.

- Have students research and prepare to defend both sides of an issue, then randomly assign them to argue for one of the positions in class or on an exam. For instance, two students might be given the assignment of researching both sides of a college-life issue, such as whether the legal drinking age should be lowered or remain the same. Before the debate begins, a flip of the coin could determine which side of the issue each student will take. As Bergquist and Phillips point out, this type of activity encourages students to "appreciate the complexity of intellectual issues and the inherent danger of simplistic thinking" (1981, p. 116).

- Have students role-play with someone with whom they disagree strongly.

Suggested Outline for Addressing Topics in Chapter 3

Step 1   Begin with a lecture launcher or icebreaker activity

Step 2   Employ a variety of classroom activities

   a. Use the PowerPoint presentation
   b. Expand on key lesson themes
   c. Involve students in a group activity
   d. Involve peer leaders
   e. Engage students in learning through case studies

Step 3   Review

   a. Address common questions and concerns about the topic
   b. Writing reflection
   d. Prepare for next class

Expanded Lesson Plan

Step 1   Lecture Launchers and Icebreakers

- Instead of immediately suggesting solutions for college adjustment challenges, first put yourself in the problem situation as if you were a student, and think through the process of solving the problem out loud. This enables you to model critical thinking for your students and allows them to witness the process of problem solving in addition to its final product. You could even ask students to bring college-adjustment dilemmas to class for you to think through and attempt to resolve in front of them. A variation of this procedure would be for you to role-play a scene involving common critical-thinking errors, and then replay the scene with the characters displaying effective critical thinking skills.

- If you have the ability to project the Internet in your classroom, consider evaluating Web pages to illustrate the process of critical thinking. A controversial issue—say, creationism versus evolution—will yield several pages that present each side as the only "truth." A valuable site is Martin Luther King, Jr.: A True Historical Examination (**www.martinlutherking.org/**). At first glance, it appears to be a scholarly study of the work of the civil rights leader. A deeper reading, however, reveals its strong biases. Ask your students which critical thinking skills they used to deduce whether or not a site is an objective, valid source. You may also get into a discussion about the ethics of presentation: Is it fair for a site to present itself as a scholarly work when it's really propaganda?

Step 2   Classroom Activities

a.   *Use the PowerPoint presentations to complement your mini-lecture.*

b.   *Key Lesson Themes*

- Pose questions to students that provoke critical thinking.

  Alison King has conducted research that shows that students can learn to generate their own higher-level thinking questions. Using a technique that she calls "guided peer questioning," students are provided with a series of generic question stems that prompt different forms of critical thinking, such as:

  What would happen if _____?
  What is the difference between _____ and _____?
  What are the implications of _____?
  Why is _____ important?
  What is another way to look at _____?" (King, 1995).

- Discuss common critical-thinking errors.

c.   *Group Activities*

- Use the following exercise to examine the four aspects of critical thinking through practical application:
  1. Form groups of four students. Each student in each group should be placed in charge of one of the four critical-thinking stages. They will record a list of examples of their particular stage based on the classroom experiences of all four students, adding how each particular experience helps make learning more meaningful for them.

2. Issue the following instructions to each group: Consider several courses you are taking now. In a group, discuss the following issues. Compare your classroom experiences with different instructors in terms of:

- **Forming Abstractions.** Do they expect or encourage students to raise questions? Do they present evidence and challenge you to interpret it? Do they challenge class members to restate or paraphrase the main idea of a lecture?
- **Creative Thinking.** Do they help you practice looking at several sides of an issue? Do they ask for your ideas on an issue? Do they ask you to keep an open mind on a question that you at first think has an obvious right answer? Do they use brainstorming strategies in which ideas can be generated without being prejudged?
- **Systematic Thinking.** Do they give you practice in following a careful line of reasoning? Do they ask you to fill in the missing steps in an argument? Do they ask you to judge whether an idea is adequately supported by logic or data?
- **Communication.** Do they have a process for encouraging students to speak — even shy students? Do they ask a member of the class to clarify a point for the benefit of other students? Have you volunteered an idea? Have you made an effort to keep an open mind about something about which you already had a strong opinion? Have you participated in a group or classroom brainstorming effort? Have you talked with the instructor before or after class or during office hours? Have you discussed ideas from the course or asked questions of other students in the class?

3. Bring groups together after 20 minutes and put the final lists on the board. Ask how such experiences facilitated their learning.

d. *Peer Leader Assistance*
- See exercise above

e. *Case Studies*

MICHEL

Michel crashed through the doorway of his residence hall room and slammed the door. "I hate women!" he yelled to his roommate, Karl. Karl asked him what was wrong. Michel sneered. "I just don't understand them. Women. Toni just broke our date for Friday night just because she found out I was drunk out of my mind at the ball game. Don't I have a right to have fun sometimes? And why should what I do when I'm out with the boys have anything to do with what goes on between Toni and me?" Karl opened his mouth to say something but Michel raised his right hand. "Shut it, Karl. Nothing you say is gonna change my mind about this."

Discussion Questions

1. How is Michel responding? What is the basis for his arguments?
2. What kind of critical-thinking errors is Michel making?
3. What are the implications of what Karl might say?
4. What is another way to look at Michel's situation?

SUSANNAH

Susannah has to write an argument essay for her freshman composition class. She chooses underage drinking as her topic. Initially, Susannah plans to argue that the drinking age should be raised to 25. In high school, Susannah's friend Tia was killed when an 18-year-old drunk driver flipped his car and sent Tia's over a guardrail. But as Susannah researches her topic, she finds information about alcohol abuse and incidents of drunk driving in other countries where the drinking age is even lower than it is in the United States. She starts to wonder if it is Americans' attitudes toward alcohol that is the problem and not the drinking age itself. Writing the paper becomes frustrating since Susannah no longer knows what thesis she is trying to prove.

Discussion Questions

1. Which general thinking skills is Susannah employing in her research?
2. Which skills could she utilize to try to clarify her stance on the issue?
3. What kind of thesis statement could Susannah write that would incorporate both sides of the issue and yet still make a strong argument for or against something?

Step 3   Review

a.   *Address Common Questions and Concerns of First-Year Students*

- *The professor says this might be right or that might be right. Why doesn't he just tell us which one?*
  Answer: Many professors are more concerned about how students arrive at an answer rather than if it is right or not. Explain and demonstrate to students that there are times when there is more than one correct answer.

- *I came to college to learn from the experts. Why do I have to listen to other students discuss a topic in class? It's such a waste of my time!*
  Answer: Participating in class discussion is a good way to gather information and listen to others' opinions. Help students realize that class discussions are a good way to develop critical-thinking and active-learning skills.

- *I don't see why I have to check so many sources in order to write a paper on one topic. Isn't one person's opinion enough?*
  Answer: Students need to learn that checking sources helps them to develop not only critical-thinking skills, but research skills too. There is often more than one theory or opinion about a topic. It is also a good way for students to learn about a topic as a "whole." Explain to students that this gives them a chance to gather evidence and consider alternatives.

- *Why do I have to explain why I think something is right? Isn't just saying it's right enough?*
  Answer: Explaining information and supporting evidence is a must for students to learn. This skill is not only important in college, but will prove to be an important life tool. Class is a good time to practice how to precisely communicate your ideas to others. Whether in school, at work, or home, they will be asked to do this over and over again.

b.   *Writing Reflection*

- Assign a one-minute paper or reaction paper at the end of class that asks students if there was any point made or position taken during the day's session that they strongly question or challenge, and then use their responses as springboards for discussion in the next class session.

Test Questions

Multiple Choice

Choose ONE answer per question.

1. Which one of the following statements is NOT good advice for developing effective thinking and writing habits?
   a. Be willing to say, "I don't know."
   b. Get used to clarifying what you mean and asking others to do so.
   c. Try to adopt the attitude that you must win every argument.
   d. Judge an argument on its merits rather than on the basis of who said it.

2. A critical thinker will do all of the following EXCEPT
   a. analyze a problem.
   b. imagine solutions, weigh them by rational criteria, and commit to one.
   c. create a simplistic analysis of a compounded issue.
   d. practice tolerance for ambiguity and complexity.

3. In college, the term *argument* refers to
   a. a physical confrontation.
   b. an emotional confrontation.
   c. a formal complaint you file against your professor.
   d. a collection of reasons and information that form logical support of some idea.

4. Chances are when you land a job, your employer is going to be more interested in how well you _____ than in how well you can memorize information.
   a. dress   c. write
   b. budget   d. think

5. Abstract thinking
   a. organizes the possibilities.
   b. uses details to discover a bigger idea.
   c. seeks connections.
   d. none of the above

6. When evaluating information on the Internet, ask yourself the following:
   a. Is it credible?
   b. Who is the author?
   c. Does it reflect mainstream opinions?
   d. all of the above

True/False

7. A strong argument appeals to your emotions the most.

8. Employers are more interested in how well you can think than in how well you can memorize information.

Short Answer

9. Name the four aspects of critical thinking.

10. Name three components of a strong argument.

Essay

11. Think about the courses you are taking this term and discuss how each one encourages each of the four aspects of critical thinking.

12. Explore the process of creative thinking. Begin by describing what defines creative thinking. Then, choose an idea and demonstrate your creative thoughts about it.

13. Explore why critical thinking is at the core of a liberal education.

14. Identify a newsworthy item that is clearly polarizing the population. Defend both positions.

15. Using the nine C's for evaluating Internet resources, critique an Internet article to be distributed by your instructor.

Answer Key

1. c, p. 31
2. c, pp. 28–29
3. d, p. 29
4. d, pp. 28–29
5. b, p. 30
6. d, p. 35
7. false, p. 30
8. true, p. 29

Web Resources

Education is Not Found in a Book   www.higher-ed.org/AEQ/if-ju.htm
Introduce this essay, written by a student at the University of South Carolina, to your class. It talks about how college provides opportunities to develop critical thinking skills—and how these opportunities mean very little if students aren't willing to put in the work.

Tutorial in Critical Reasoning   commhum.mccneb.edu/argument/summary.htm
This interactive tutorial will help students identify the argument of an essay as well as recognize structure and search for conclusions. Additional writing exercises are included on the site.

Intro to Creative Thinking   www.virtualsalt.com/crebook1.htm
Take a look at this extensive article, written by Robert Harris, author of *Creative Problem Solving: A Step-by-Step* Approach. It covers everything from myths about creative thinking to positive attitudes for creativity.

Collaborative Learning   scholar.lib.vt.edu/ejournals/JTE/jte-v7n1/gokhale.jte-v7n1.html
This study, originally published in the *Journal of Technology Education,* focuses on how collaborative learning enhances critical thinking. A fascinating read.

Decision Making Skills   www.hooah4health.com/spirit/decisions.htm

For More Information

Bartholomew, R. E. and Radford, B. (2003). *Hoaxes, myths, and mania: Why we need critical thinking.* New York: Prometheus Books.

DiSpezio, M. A. (1997). *Great critical thinking puzzles.* New York: Sterling Publishing.

Glasser, E. M. (1941). *An experiment in the development of critical thinking.* New York: AMS Press.

Toulmin, S. E. (1958). *The uses of argument.* New York: Cambridge University Press.

Walter, T. L. (2003). *Critical thinking: Building the basics* (2nd ed). San Francisco: Wadsworth Publishing.

4 Maximizing Your Learning Success

Engaging with Learning and
Making the Most of Your Learning Style

Chapter Objectives:

1. To introduce students to the concept of being an engaged and collaborative learner and how these qualities help students learn more effectively and enjoy their college experience more
2. To teach students the strategies they can use to form high-quality learning teams
3. To discuss how study groups are particularly helpful for science and math class
4. To teach students how to work effectively with instructors
5. To help students discover their own learning styles and how to apply the results to studying and learning
6. To help students understand and recognize a learning disability in themselves and others

Timing of Chapter Coverage

For the sake of concentration of effort and continuity, you might want to teach this chapter after you have taught Chapter 2 on Managing Time and Staying Motivated.

About This Chapter

This chapter can be valuable in showing students that study skills can be linked to an awareness of how they learn. If they know their strengths, they can develop study skills to help them compensate for their weaknesses. Some first-year students believe a mystery surrounds the success of some students and the failure of others—that there's a kind of magic that successful students have. You know this isn't true. By teaching study skills in general and addressing learning styles, you can help demystify success and failure, provide a series of methods that will encourage being a more deliberate and organized student, and facilitate the students' self-development.

For many students, the term *engagement with learning* is a foreign concept. There is an abundance of research and scholarship to support the importance of actively involving students in the learning process. This chapter provides for students a rationale for the value of becoming engaged in the learning process and offers strategies to accomplish this. Since the authors believe so completely in active learning, we recommend that as instructors you strive to employ as many active learning devices as you can throughout the first-year seminar course:

- Ask students for feedback regularly, read their remarks, and respond to them.

- Employ the "one-minute paper" at the end of class: What was the most important issue of today's class? What is the unanswered question you have about today's class? The answers will prepare you to reach your students the next day.

- Encourage students to get to know their teachers. A suggestion: Challenge each student to interview the teacher he or she likes least. Students may only confirm their dislike in some cases, but in others they may find a different individual sitting across the desk from them.

- Help students understand that there are no "dumb questions." Challenge them to ask the questions that nobody else in the room wants to ask because they think the instructor will laugh at them, even though they need answers.

This is a wonderful opportunity to introduce students to elements of collaboration as a way to maximize their learning success. Work through several of the exercises and give students the opportunity to develop learning teams for this class.

This chapter also highlights the importance of fostering the instructor-student relationship. No other course will probably address this issue with students, so it is imperative they recognize that having a positive relationship with an instructor may be a critical part of the learning process in college.

Suggested Outline for Addressing Topics in Chapter 4

Step 1   Begin with a lecture launcher or icebreaker activity

Step 2   Employ a variety of classroom activities
   a. Use the PowerPoint presentation
   b. Expand on key lesson themes
   c. Involve students in group activity
   d. Involve peer leaders
   e. Engage students in learning through case studies

Step 3   Review
   a. Address common questions and concerns about the topic
   b. Writing reflection

Expanded Lesson Plan

Step 1   Lecture Launchers and Icebreakers
- Use these instructions to present an exercise that focuses on the different ways people acquire information. Follow the script and directions with the class:

   "I am going to ask you as a class to all do one action and then freeze. Are you ready? Do this and then freeze. Look at your fingernails. Leave your hands frozen and look up at me. Now use one of your hands to raise your hand to respond to one of these questions. How many held out your hands, palm down, fingers pointed away, looking at your nails and the back of your hand?" (Draw on the board a rough figure of a hand and fingers extended. Draw in the nails.)

   "Raise your hand if you did this." (Demonstrate.) *Count the number and write it on the board by the figure.* "Thank you. Hands down."

   "Now, how many curled your fingers back over your palm and looked at your nails?" (Draw this figure.) *"Raise your hand if you did this."* (Demonstrate.) *Count this number and write it on the board.* "Thank you. Hands down."

"Finally, how many of you just looked at your fingernails without moving your hands at all?" Count again and write this number on the board. "Okay, unfreeze."

"Here I am, your instructor. I asked my class to do a simple task, and I got different responses. What suggestions can you give me?" From here, the discussion can follow in many directions such as how we all differ, how you might differ from your instructor, and different personality types. A student may ask, "What is the right answer?" This opens up discussion that many questions in college classes may not have only one answer. You can explain to the students that faculty may be more interested in how a student arrived at the answer, no matter what it is.

Exercise written by C. B. Red Bright, Jackson State Community College, Jackson, TN.

- Ask students to jot down their answer to this question: "A meeting scheduled for 10:30 has been moved up 30 minutes. What time does the meeting start?" Pause for a moment and then repeat, "Moved up 30 minutes. What time does the meeting start?" Count the answers for both 10:00 and 11:00, and discuss the differences with your students. Have the differing "sides" defend their answers, and explain that it all hinges on the word *up* in time. Encourage students to analyze why *up* in time means that to them. Don't accept, "That's just want it means." Emphasize the importance of vocabulary and of asking teachers for clarification when necessary.

Step 2   Classroom Activities

a.   *Use the PowerPoint presentations to complement your mini-lecture.*

b.   *Key Lesson Themes*
- Give an explanation of the VARK Learning Style Inventory. Allow students to express their understanding of this model.
- Generate a discussion on the pros and cons of learning teams.

c.   *Group Activities*
Ask students to form groups. The following tasks will help them analyze and adjust to the different teaching styles of their instructors, to develop learning styles other than their own preferred style (i.e., less dominant learning style), and to increase the flexibility of the way they study:
- Discuss your learning style and how you have adapted to professors who teach in different styles.
- Offer strategies on how students could adapt to a professor whose teaching style does not match their (the students') learning styles.
- Make a list of the preferred learning style of each student. Keep for further classroom assignments.

d.   *Peer Leader Assistance*
Ask your students to write a response to this question: "What is engagement with learning?" Take the time to have students read their answers to the rest of the class. It will be time well spent. You will learn if they understand the difference, and you'll probably be able to elaborate on some of the comments they make. This activity could serve as a segue into the lesson mini-lecture.

e.   *Case Studies*

KEISHA

Keisha is a first-year student taking 15 credits. She has found out that there is a lot of work required for each class. She also sees that instructors seem to have a different way of teaching their class and emphasizing the material. Keisha seems to be having the most trouble with her Philosophy class and is finding the lecture hard to follow. She got a D on the first test and is worried because she was a good student in high school. The professor discusses many aspects of the different philosophers' theories during the lecture. Keisha is having difficulty tying them together and is more in tune with the names of key figures, dates, and major points. Her next test is in two weeks.

Discussion Questions

1. Why is Keisha having this difficulty?
2. What can she do to improve her situation?
3. What can Keisha do to better understand each lecture?
4. How can Keisha best prepare for her next exam?

HOWIE

Howie's lab partner, Kai, has a particular way of completing each assignment. She is thorough and methodical, and she seems to have an immediate grasp of all new material they are learning in class. Howie, however, needs more time to digest the concepts they're studying. Kai becomes very critical and impatient with Howie whenever he asks her a question. Clearly, Kai prefers working by herself than with another person. As a result, Kai often completes the assignments with little input from Howie. Howie feels that Kai's interference keeps him from fully learning the material covered by each lab assignment. His mother has suggested he speak to his professor about this problem, but Howie doesn't want to sound like a complainer.

Discussion Questions

1. What psychological types would you assess to both Howie and Kai?
2. How could Howie work with his learning style to improve his relationship with Kai?
3. If you were Howie, what would you do: go to your professor or work things out with Kai on your own?

Step 3   Review

a.   *Address Common Questions and Concerns of First-Year Students*

- *How can you put people in these little boxes?*
  Answer: Students should be encouraged to understand psychological types. Have them try the self-assessment on page 44 to see where they stand.

- *I'm eighteen years old. How can I change my learning style now?*
  Answer: Encourage students to work on their strengths while exploring other learning styles.

- *Is one learning style better than another?*
  Answer: The book does not try to privilege any one style over the other. However, students should be aware of the preferred learning styles for acquiring information to be a doctor, lawyer, or teacher.

- *Why do I really need to develop a wider range of learning styles?*
  Answer: To be successful in college, students will need a great variety of skills. Really emphasize the importance of understanding the differences in kinesthetic, analytical, auditory, and other learning styles.

- *Will my learning style really be relevant to anything after I graduate from college?*
  Answer: Stress to your students that they are developing life-long skills.

- *What difference do learning styles make in job situations?*
  Answer: Just as groups can be enhanced with people who have different learning styles, so can the workplace.

b.   *Writing Reflection*

- Choose one or more of the reflection questions on page 49 in the text and ask students to respond in writing.

Test Questions

Multiple Choice

Choose ONE answer per question.

1. *Engagement* means
   a. active involvement in every aspect of life.
   b. approaching every challenge with determination.
   c. a and b
   d. none of the above

2. There is/are _____ learning style models
   a. only one   c. five
   b. two   d. numerous

3. According to the text, when forming a learning team, you should NOT
   a. seek peers who are different than you in terms of cultural background.
   b. keep the group large (seven or more students).
   c. hold individual team members accountable for their own learning.
   d. hold individual team members accountable for contributing to the learning of their teammates.

4. If you are unsatisfied with a grade you received on a recent paper, the first thing you should do is
   a. file a complaint within the department.
   b. ask your teacher if you can redo the assignment.
   c. ask another instructor within the same department to look at your paper and offer a second opinion.
   d. speak with your teacher about why you received the grade you did.

5. In a ground breaking study on factors predicting success in calculus, it was determined that the most effective strategy for success in calculus turned out to be
   a. active participation in a study group.
   b. individualized learning.
   c. a and b
   d. none of the above

True/False

6. If you cannot resolve a situation with an instructor, the first thing you should do is go to the department head.

7. You learn from your fellow classmates as well as from your instructors.

Short Answer

8. List some simple things you can do to improve relations between you and your teachers.

9. Name three benefits of active learning.

10. What does the acronym VARK mean?

Essay

11. Imagine a world in which everyone had the same learning style as you. How would life be better? How might it be worse? Explain your answers fully.

12. How can knowing your VARK score help you do better in your college classes? Now that you know your VARK score, what changes do you propose to make in how you study and why?

13. Identify one of your present instructors whose teaching style conflicts with your learning style. Outline in detail some changes that you plan to make to ensure that you make a good grade in this class.

14. If you suspect you have a learning disability, develop a plan of action on how you will address this and ensure that you make a good GPA your first semester in college.

15. Think of a time when you've had a conflict with a teacher. What was the conflict? What was your role in it? The teacher's role? How was the conflict resolved? Is there anything you would do differently today?

Answer Key
1. c, p. 38
2. d, p. 38
3. b, p. 40
4. d, p. 43

5. a, p. 41
6. false, p. 43
7. true, p. 40

Web Resources

Index of Learning Styles Questionnaire   www.engr.ncsu.edu/learningstyles/ilsweb.html
The ILS offered on this page was authored by Barbara A. Solomon and Richard M. Felder. It is entirely free and is accompanied by pages explaining the different styles assessed by this questionnaire.

Relationships   www.literacynet.org/lp/learn2learn/students/relationships.html
For students interested in knowing more about how their learning styles affect their relationships, this site offers bulleted lists of qualities common among types, as well as strengths and challenges for each individual.

On Learning Styles   www.gsu.edu/~dschjb/wwwmbti.html
Georgia State University's master teaching program offers this extensive document, which provides several strategies for teaching each different type of student.

Assessment of learning modalities (visual, auditory, tactile/kinesthetic)   www.hcc.hawaii.edu/intranet/committees/FacDevCom/guidebk/teachtip/lernstyl.htm

For More Information

Avila, A. (1999). *Lovetypes: Discover your romantic style and find your soul mate.* New York: Avon.

Keirsey, D. (1998). *Please understand me II: Temperament, character, and intelligence.* Del Mar, CA: Prometheus Nemesis.

Lawrence, G. D. (1997). *Looking at type and learning styles.* Gainesville, FL: Center for Applications of Psychological Type.

Myers, I. B. and Myers, P. (1993). *Gifts differing: Understanding personality type.* Palo Alto, CA: Consulting Psychologists Press.

Smith, B. L. and McCann, J. eds. (2001). *Reinventing ourselves: Interdisciplinary education, collaborative learning, and experimentation in higher education.* Bolton, MA: Anker Pub. Co.

Tieger, P. D. and Barron-Tieger, B. (2001). *Do what you are: Discover the perfect career for you through the secrets of personality type* (3rd ed). New York: Little, Brown and Company.

5 Communicating Clearly
Writing and Speaking for Success

Chapter Objectives:

1. To demonstrate the importance of writing as a process leading to a product
2. To demonstrate how to use reviews and revisions to strengthen your writing
3. To remind students that writing an e-mail is not the same as writing a college paper
4. To illustrate how best to use body language and voice when speaking in public
5. To explain how to sound organized and composed when speaking on the spot
6. To acquaint students with six important steps in preparing a successful speech

Timing of Chapter Coverage

The writing portion of this chapter warrants attention early in the term. In fact, you might integrate the writing concepts in this chapter with the earlier chapters on study skills for the obvious reason that students who learn to put thoughts on paper clearly tend to be better at absorbing material and explaining material on tests.

The chapter also focuses on two aspects of speaking: prepared speeches and impromptu speaking. You may want to break the speaking portion into these two components and use them at separate times during the term. While it is important to get students comfortable with "informal" speaking in class immediately, this part of the chapter is probably best used around the middle of the term. First-year students often have high anxiety about formal speaking assignments, particularly at the start of the course when they do not know their classmates.

About This Chapter

Writing

You will find that first-year students tend to fall into one of three categories when it comes to writing: the deluded, the helpless, and the true writers. The deluded have received high marks on papers in high school and are convinced that there is nothing more to learn about writing. Sadly, this is often far from the case.

Many students will claim that they learned some unbreakable rules about writing that you seem to be breaking. For example: "An essay should contain only five paragraphs: a thesis statement, four points, and a conclusion." Or, "Never use the first or second person in writing." What they have missed, perhaps, is that writing style depends to a large extent on the audience one is writing for. This group will find their mediocre grades shocking and may go so far as to let you know how well they did in high school.

The helpless haven't received those high grades, and perhaps that's a blessing. While they are probably convinced that they will never be good writers, these students represent fertile territory for writing instruction. Coach them gently; along with your criticisms, find something positive to write on every paper. Be encouraging. This, of course, applies to the first group as well.

Finally, we come to the true writers. You can expect to get wonderful work from these folks who, seemingly, have overcome what may have been inadequate writing instruction and developed a style of their own. You will still find things to critique, face it, anyone's writing can always be improved. You will love reading their papers.

Be certain to introduce writing as a means of motivating thinking. Use the suggestions in the chapter to get them started. Above all, try to convince them that good writing can open doors for them throughout their lives. For example, have you ever tried to read a poorly written résumé?

Speaking

Typically, first-year students have considerable anxiety about speaking in front of others. They see public speaking as cause for extreme self-consciousness rather than as an opportunity to command the attention of others and communicate the totality of their thoughts. Normal dialogue denies speakers the full extent of these opportunities because give and take is required. Conversational speakers who command attention and monopolize the interaction are considered to be lacking in social skills. Public speakers, on the other hand, are expected to command and control. You can present these ideas as advantages of public speaking. Keep the following goals in mind in helping students manage their anxiety:

- Recast public speaking as "multiple conversations."

- Redefine public speaking as a natural part of life.

- Redirect students' anxieties for use as productive energy.

Recasting Public Speaking

Help students rethink public speaking as multiple "conversations" occurring simultaneously. Encourage students to think of themselves speaking to each individual in the class as they would during normal conversation rather than speaking to a group of people. Students often think they must play a role while speaking in front of others—a role with which they are not comfortable. Remind them that speakers should be themselves and should not play the role of orator. It's important to let their personalities shine through while speaking publicly. Simply reporting information isn't enough; audiences are interested in speakers as people.

Redefining Public Speaking

Help students understand that when we come right down to it, all speaking is public speaking. Whenever we speak, we do so in public. Few of us do much speaking in private. In other words, public speaking should be considered a continual way of life rather than a "one-shot" event.

Redirecting Anxiety

Remind students that experiencing anxiety while speaking in front of others is normal. Anxiety means that students care about what they're doing and want to do well. Anxiety can be harnessed as productive energy if they follow the advice on preparation and rehearsal presented in the chapter.

Of course, students with excessive anxiety may require extra coaching from you or a referral to the communication department or speech lab on campus if available. Like swimming, speaking is the kind of skill that can only be learned by doing. Reading about speaking and discussing how to give a speech must be combined with speaking opportunities. Keep in mind that evaluating public speaking is tricky.

Speaking is an egocentric activity, and instructors must be careful to provide helpful feedback without bruising fragile egos. Producing a speech is comparable to creating a work of art; identifying areas for improvement must be done supportively, and students' self-esteem must be protected. If the entire class is to provide feedback following speeches, it's important to set guidelines and encourage constructive rather than destructive comments from the class. Some instructors elect to provide only positive feedback in public; they communicate negative comments supportively in one-on-one coaching sessions after class. However you choose to proceed, sensitivity is key.

The most effective way to improve speaking skills is to allow students to view themselves on videotape. If you have the opportunity, videotape students' speeches yourself or have the media department or a student assistant do it. Students can see and hear speaking errors themselves and self-improvement can be dramatic.

Suggested Outline for Addressing Topics in Chapter 5

Step 1   Begin with a lecture launcher or icebreaker activity

Step 2   Employ a variety of classroom activities
a. Use PowerPoint presentation
b. Expand on key lesson themes
c. Involve students in a group activity
d. Involve peer leaders
e. Engage students in learning through case studies

Step 3   Review
a. Address common questions and concerns about the topic
b. Writing reflection
c. Prepare for next class

Expanded Lesson Plan

Step 1   Lecture Launchers and Icebreakers
- Have your students review some famous speeches, first in the written form and then in audio or video form. Have them compare both versions and analyze the strengths and possible weaknesses of each. This will not only introduce your students to the chapter material, it will provide them with a strong illustration of the importance of both the written and spoken word.

- Ask for half a dozen volunteers. Hand each one a folded slip of paper with a certain posture written on it (arms folded across chest, head tilted, and so on). Next, ask each student to repeat the same sentence (of your choosing) using the assigned posture. Have your class guess which attitude is implied by which posture. This will lead to a discussion on the importance of body language. You may also want to ask your students to decode the tone of voice used by your volunteers. For example, did they automatically adjust their normal tone to match their assigned posture?

Step 2   Classroom Activities

a.   *Use the PowerPoint presentations to complement your mini-lecture.*

b.   *Expand on key lesson themes*

FREEWRITING

To get students into the habit of using freewriting, open the class meeting with a short freewriting session (perhaps five minutes) on a topic related to the chapter. Continue to do this week after week to encourage students to regularly reflect on the reading, the course, and their own perspectives.

USING VIDEO TO IMPROVE STUDENT SPEECHES

In preparation for this chapter, have each student choose a topic on which to give a short speech. On the day that students deliver the speeches, use a camcorder to record them. The following session, ask your students what makes for a successful speech. Decide as a class which criteria are most important. Next, play the video for your class.

c.   *Group Activities*
   - Using recorded video, have the students critique each speech on the basis of the criteria they decided on. As a final step, you may ask each student to write a brief response to the entire process—from delivering the speech to having it critiqued by fellow classmates. Ask them to assess their strengths and weakness as a speechmaker. This can be an eye-opener for many students. If they are willing, have them turn their papers in or read them to the class. More importantly, collect the papers they wrote about the experience. Ask them to share the papers with the rest of the class and to come to some conclusion about the relative value of the exercise and how they might use it to improve their public speaking.

d.   *Peer Leader Assistance*
   - In addition to actively participating in the activities surrounding this topic, peer leaders should ensure that props and logical arrangements for these activities are scheduled in advance.

a. *Case Studies*

DAPHNE

In high school, Daphne excelled in English, earning mostly A's on her papers. She had a knack for figuring out what teachers wanted to read and knew how to deliver the material in a clean, articulate fashion. Daphne wasn't all that concerned when her first big essay was assigned in her freshman composition class. She started the paper three nights before it was due, finished it the following day, and turned the essay in early. She was confident that she would receive another A.

When she got her essay back, however, Daphne was dismayed to see that she had only earned a C. Her instructor's comments noted a lack of original thought, disorganized structure, and several typos as the reasons for the lower-than-expected grade. Daphne was crushed. Why were her usual writing methods failing her now? When the next essay came up, Daphne found herself paralyzed by fear. She didn't know what to write or how to write it. On top of that, she wasn't sure how she should structure the paper once she chose a topic. Eventually, she "borrowed" a topic from her roommate. After waiting until the night before the paper was due, Daphne repeated the process she used on the first paper, hoping this time her instructor would be more generous with the grades.

Discussion Questions

1. What were some of the things Daphne did wrong in writing the first paper? The second?
2. What steps should Daphne take if she truly wants to write A papers?
3. How could Daphne have better prepared herself for that second paper? Have you ever had writer's block? What did you do to get over it?

JAKE

For his college success course, Jake was assigned to do a ten-minute PowerPoint presentation on his research topic. He had three weeks to prepare—a good length of time. He projected his schedule for the next three weeks in his head. In addition to soccer finals, his parents were flying in for a visit, and the following week his high school girlfriend was driving up for a visit as well. Along with his other classes, these important events were likely to take up some time. But Jake wasn't concerned. He made a mental note to run some topic ideas by his father and to ask his girlfriend (who was a whiz at PowerPoint) for some help.

Despite Jake's "planning," the days clicked by, visits came and went, and the speech never seemed to get done. Jake had never considered himself to be very good at public speaking, and the thought of taking on such a big project was overwhelming. The night before, he went through a few last-minute motions doing Internet research and putting together a few slides. It wasn't a valiant attempt; in fact, Jake knew it was some of the worst work he'd ever done. But he was finished, and that was what mattered most in Jake's head.

Discussion Questions

1. Have you ever felt as Jake did in this case study? What was worrying Jake? In your own experience, what worried you?
2. Why does procrastination sometimes appear to be such an attractive option? What kinds of things do we tell ourselves about doing the work later?
3. Was fear an issue in Jake's procrastination? Should Jake have gone to his professor and explained his fear of public speaking?
4. If you had been Jake, what would you have done to make the project less threatening and more manageable?

Step 3   Review

a.   *Address Common Questions and Concerns of First-Year Students*

- *I already know how to write. Why do I have to practice an approach that I don't like?*
  Answer: Writing is a powerful tool of communication. It's also a skill students will need for the rest of their lives. The approach taught in this chapter emphasizes organization and revision, two steps most first-year students think they can skip. Explain to students that even published authors use this process. You must also impress upon them that no matter how brilliant they are as students, if they do not know how to articulate their thoughts both in writing and verbally, no one will be able to measure just how brilliant they are.

- *I'll never be a good writer. My major is math (or science, or engineering, or . . .) and I won't need to write.*
  Answer: Again, writing is a basic life skill. Although students who are oriented toward math and sciences may never grow to love the writing process, they must learn to master it. To convert skeptical students, give them examples of how good writing skills are an asset in math- and science-related careers. You may also try to relate the writing process to something they are more comfortable with, such as a formula. By doing this, you are demystifying the writing process and making it more accessible to these students.

- *Why do I have to know how to give a speech? I'm not planning on being a politician.*
  Answer: Being able to articulate thoughts verbally is every bit as important as being able to do so in writing. Again, make sure your students are aware of how good speaking skills will aid them in practical ways such as on job interviews.

- *When I give a speech, my heart pounds and my knees knock. How can I keep from being nervous?*
  Answer: Fear of public speaking is natural, especially among first-year students. Review "Becoming a Better Public Speaker" (pages 58–59) and "Six Steps to Better Public Speaking" (pages 60–61).

- *Should I memorize my speech? What kind of notes do I need?*
  Answer: Memorizing a speech often leads to a flat delivery. It is better for students to create an outline of key points they want to cover and practice, practice, practice. The more they say the words—especially if they use their friends and classmates as an audience—the more natural the actual speech will sound. This kind of practice should also help reduce their level of anxiety.

- *Why can't I just speak off the top of my head? I hate speeches that sound "canned."*
  Answer: Like any piece of good writing, a strong speech relies heavily on pre-planning. The text does not suggest that students should write out a speech, memorize it, and then deliver to their audience. It does, however, advocate a six-step process of preparation. Illustrate for your students how even a minimal amount of planning can improve their speaking skills.

b.   *Writing Reflection*
Leave a few minutes at the end of class for students to complete the Portfolio section on page 63.

Test Questions

Multiple Choice

Choose ONE answer per question.

1. According to your text, writing serves two purposes, exemplified in the terms _____ writing and _____ writing.
    a. communicative; descriptive
    c. exploratory; explanatory
    b. creative; scientific
    d. creative; concrete

2. Many writing experts believe that the writing step that should take the longest is
    a. prewriting or rehearsing.
    c. rewriting or revision.
    b. writing or drafting.
    d. none of the above

3. This is when exploratory writing becomes a rough explanatory draft.
    a. Rewriting or revision
    c. Prewriting or rehearsing
    b. Writing or drafting
    d. none of the above

4. What's the first thing you should do when planning a successful speech?
    a. Prepare your notes
    c. Organize your information
    b. Analyze your audience
    d. Clarify your objective

5. When visual aids are added to a presentation, listeners
    a. can absorb and recall more information.
    b. tend to become distracted and tune out.
    c. rate the presenter as more knowledgeable.
    d. view the presenter as cold and distant.

6. According to the text, a writer should spend _____ percent on the prewriting (including research and thinking) stage.
    a. 55
    c. 75
    b. 65
    d. 85

7. Which is NOT one of the six steps to successful speaking?
    a. Analyze your information
    c. Prepare your notes
    b. Organize your information
    d. Practice your delivery

8. According to the text, a writer should spend _____ percent of his time on the writing (first draft) stage.
    a. 10
    c. 1
    b. 5
    d. none of the above

9. When using notes to give a speech, the best speaking aid is a
    a. minimal outline.
    c. sketchy outline.
    b. detailed outline.
    d. none of the above

Short Answer

10. What are the three stages of writing? Give your answer in the order of which step you spend the least time on to the one you spend the most time on.

11. Name the three most widely used forms of supporting materials.

12. List three ways you can practice your delivery.

13. List five questions to ask yourself when analyzing your audience.

14. What are three guidelines to follow as you select your visuals for a speech?

Essay

15. Define the difference between exploratory writing and explanatory writing, and tell why it is important to go through one stage before moving to the other.

16. Imagine that your instructor assigns a ten-minute speech on a topic of your choice. Choose your topic, identify the six steps to success discussed in this chapter, and write about how you would complete each step in order to create the best presentation possible.

17. What was the most important lesson you learned from this chapter? Why is this so?

18. What behaviors are you planning to change after reading this chapter? Why?

Answer Key

1. c, p. 54	6. d, p. 56
2. a, p. 56	7. a, p. 60
3. b, p. 56	8. c, p. 57
4. d, p. 60	9. a, p. 61
5. a, p. 61	

Web Resources

Prewriting Exercises   students.faulkner.edu/cwalker/Comp1/prewriting_exercises.htm
Most college students don't take the time to complete any prewriting exercises. Direct them to this site, which offers some quick but valuable prewriting exercises your students can employ on their next papers.

Revising Your Paper for Content   alpha.furman.edu/~moakes/Powerwrite/revise.htm
For some college students, revising means running spell check. This page debunks that myth and explains how students can revise their papers to improve content. It also contains a link to a section that does deal with revising for mechanics.

Great American Speeches   www.pbs.org/greatspeeches/
This rich resource affiliated with PBS not only contains speech texts, it also offers background information on each speaker as well as several audio and video links. This site would be useful if you're planning on trying out Lecture Launcher 1.

Conquer Public Speaking Fear   www.stresscure.com/jobstress/speak.html
This inspiring site features best-selling author Dr. Morton C. Orman who offers 11 principles to overcoming the fear of public speaking.

Student Journal Writing   www.ericfacility.net/databases/ERIC_Digests/ed378587.html
This report, compiled by the Educational Resources Information Center (ERIC), lists different styles of student journals and discusses the effectiveness of each. It's particularly useful to instructors who have never incorporated journaling into their coursework.

AmeriCorps   www.americorps.org/
The homepage for AmeriCorps, one of the highest-profile networks of national service programs, boasts testimonials, research reports, and information on how to join and/or create new programs.

Public speaking   www.selfgrowth.com/public.html
www.school-for-champions. com/speaking/resources.htm

For More Information

Carnegie, D. (1990). *The quick and easy way to effective speaking.* New York: Prentice Hall.

Coburn, K. L. and Treeger, M. L. (2003). *Letting go: A parents' guide to understanding the college years* (4th ed). New York: Quill William Morrow.

Esposito, J. E. (2000). *In the spotlight: Overcome your fear of public speaking and performing.* New York: HarperCollins.

Kaye, C. B. (2003). *The complete guide to service learning: Proven, practical ways to engage students in civic responsibility, academic curriculum, and social action.* Minneapolis: Free Spirit Press.

Seligman, M. E. (2007). *What you can change and what you can't: The complete guide to successful self-improvement.* New York: Vintage.

6 Listening, Note Taking, and Participating in Class
Committing to Classroom Success

Chapter Objectives

1. To demonstrate how to listen critically to lectures and class discussions
2. To help students assess and improve their note-taking skills
3. To illustrate how good class notes can help students do their homework
4. To encourage students to prepare before class
5. To discuss why it is important to review notes soon after class
6. To explain how to review class and textbook materials after class
7. To demonstrate how to take notes in math and science courses
8. To encourage students to speak up in class

Timing of Chapter Coverage

You may find that this chapter is best taught after Chapter 4, "Maximizing Your Learning Success." In many courses, students begin falling behind the very first day of class if they do not have an efficient method of taking lecture notes. The information in this chapter will provide students with strategies for not only getting involved in class, but also with ways to gather important classroom information. First-year students need to learn how to "cope" in the classroom environment and adapt to lectures as quickly as possible. This chapter's information can help them do just that.

About This Chapter

Students are likely to comment that in contrast to many high school classes, which are focused on a textbook, many college classes are focused on the lectures and the textbook may be supportive rather than primary. Because of this essential difference, college students must listen attentively to lectures and write down both main ideas and supporting details in ways that are clear, comprehensive, and conducive to learning and recall later on. If they do not listen and take effective notes, there may not be a textbook to fall back on like there was in high school.

As a rule, testing is fairly frequent in high school. It is usually much less frequent in college. In fact, at some schools, instructors of first-year courses test only twice during the term and once during finals. Consequently, there are long periods of time between the delivery of the information and the demonstration of knowledge. This suggests, once again, the importance of accurate and effective note taking.

Having a note-taking system is paramount to a student's success in the classroom. This chapter gives specific strategies for before, during, and after class as well as class participation. Make sure students know these strategies and can determine how they will improve their classroom experience and overall learning.

Suggested Outline for Addressing Topics in Chapter 6

Step 1   Begin with a lecture launcher or icebreaker activity

Step 2   Employ a variety of classroom activities

a. Use the PowerPoint presentation
b. Expand on key lesson themes
c. Involve students in a group activity
d. Involve peer leaders
e. Engage students in learning through case studies

Step 3   Review

a. Address common questions and concerns about the topic
b. Writing reflection
c. Prepare for next class

Expanded Lesson Plan

Step 1   Lecture Launchers and Icebreakers

- You may want to begin by asking students to discuss how college classes are structured differently from high school classes and how they are adjusting to this transition. Examining these differences may help to bridge the gaps they are experiencing as new students. Ask them to consider and discuss some of the following questions:
  - How are they adjusting to the transition in the classroom?
  - Are some college classes easier to take notes in? Why?
  - What does the instructor do to facilitate students' understanding of lectures?
  - What does the instructor do to make it easy to take notes?
  - What strategies can make note taking easier?
- Ask students to share with their partners any difficulties they are experiencing with lectures. From there, you can begin to discuss student experiences in the classroom with lectures, note taking, and participation. This will give you a place to start as well as evaluate your students' skill levels.

Step 2   Classroom Activities

a. *Use the PowerPoint presentations to complement your mini-lecture.*

b. *Key Lesson Themes*

TESTING MEMORY

1. Ask your students to think back to a lecture they heard in another class the day before.
2. Have them jot down as many main ideas and supporting details as they can remember.
3. As part of a homework assignment or in class, have students compare these lists to the notes they took in that class.
4. Students quickly realize how incomplete their lists are. This activity demonstrates more clearly than any lecture could how important it is to review.

EFFECTIVE NOTE TAKING:
DISCUSS AND DEMONSTRATE THE CORNELL SYSTEM OF NOTE TAKING

1. Ask your students to take notes on this lecture. Afterward, give them an additional ten minutes to fill in the recall column.

2. Next, have students pair up to compare the most important ideas presented in the lecture. Have them discuss whether reading the assignment prior to the lecture informed their note-taking abilities.

3. An alternative is to instruct your students not to take notes on the lecture. Then deliver another mini-lecture of equal difficulty, but this time, instruct the students to take notes. During your next class meeting, quiz them on both lectures to demonstrate that their recall of the second lecture was greater.

c.   *Group Activities*

- Ask students to take out the notebook they use for this or any other class. Pair them up and have them show one page of their notes to their partner. Let each partner see if they can "make sense" of this page of notes. They can give feedback on the following:

  - Can they understand the general idea of the notes?
  - Can they identify the topic of the lecture?
  - How do the notes look to them?

Show the students a sample of how you take notes and discuss with the students the strengths and weakness of your note-taking style.

d.   *Peer Leader Assistance*

Facilitate the group exercise.

e. *Case Studies*

NATE

Nate is a first-year student. He has had difficulty concentrating during the first week of lectures in his economics class and already seems to be losing his focus in his other classes. Listening to lectures and taking notes is extremely difficult for him. He's finding that his notes do not make sense and he seems to be lacking important lecture information. At the end of the first week, he meets with his economics professor during office hours. He then proceeds to tell the professor that when he was in elementary school he was diagnosed with Attention Deficit Hyperactivity Disorder (ADHD). He confides that he has been taking medication and getting some additional assistance from teachers with note taking and studying for tests, beginning in elementary school and right up through high school.

Discussion Questions
1. What suggestions would you make to help Nate?
2. What strategies do you have that might help Nate in other classes?
3. What ways could instructors adjust their teaching style to assist students like Nate?
4. What other ways could the instructor help Nate?

RITA

Rita has recently returned to college and started taking night classes. After high school, she started working full-time in a law firm to make money, gain experience, and see if she would be interested in pursuing law school. She works full time during the day and lives at home with her parents. Rita's night classes are long and she is usually very tired from her workday when she gets there. All Rita can seem to do is sit back in her lectures and take notes. She feels too tired to ask questions and participate in class activities. She knows that class participation counts for 20 percent of her grade in one class. Rita knows she can pass the class with at least a C by doing this, but it is not her best effort. She is trying to get good grades now so when she applies to law school, she will have a competitive GPA. Rita wants to get A's in her classes.

Discussion Questions
1. What are Rita's issues in this situation?
2. What strategies would you suggest Rita use in the classroom?
3. What strategies outside the classroom would you suggest for Rita?
4. How can Rita motivate herself to participate in class and in her learning?
5. How can Rita become a more active learner?

Step 3   Review

a.   *Address Common Questions and Concerns of First-Year Students*

- *Why do I need to take notes? I can just read the text.*
  Answer: Just reading the text is not enough to effectively learn class material. Many times instructors present lecture material that supplements the textbook. Students need to realize that they may miss important information if they do not take notes.

- *Why do I have to take notes? I like to sit back and enjoy the lecture, and taking notes gets in the way.*
  Answer: Effective learning takes place when students are actively engaged with the lecture material. Explain to them some of the differences between active and passive students in the classroom (if you have not yet covered Chapter 4, "Engagement with Learning"). Remind them that note taking enhances active listening, furthers their absorption of the material, and provides more structure to test preparation.

- *Why can't I just bring in a tape recorder?*
  Answer: While recording a lecture may be helpful in some ways, it may not be as effective as the student anticipates. Tell students that recording a lecture often ensures that they will sit through it at least twice. This can be extremely time consuming. Encourage students to find other ways to get lecture information. However, if there's a reason students need to tape the lecture (commuters for example, may want to take advantage of listening to the taped lectures during their commute), remind them to ask their instructor's permission before doing so.

- *How can I take notes when he/she talks too fast?*
  Answer: Students sometimes run into this problem. First, remind them that they do not have to write down everything a professor says. Encourage them to explore other methods of filling in their notes, such as meeting with the professor or forming a study group to compare notes.

- *Should I take notes during a discussion?*
  Answer: Discussions are a part of active learning. Encourage students to write down key points and discussions. They may need to correlate discussion notes with their lecture notes, as well as determine their importance to the class material. Remind students that they may be responsible for the information presented during a discussion session on a later test.

- *If an outline is presented, should I copy it all down at the beginning of the lecture?*
  Answer: Encourage students to copy an outline as it's presented so they don't miss important lecture information.

b.   *Writing Reflection*

- Give students a few minutes to do the Portfolio exercise on page 75.

Test Questions

Multiple Choice

Choose ONE answer per question.

1. You should record a teacher's lecture.
    a. as long as it is less than 30 minutes.
    b. after receiving permission from the instructor.
    c. only for small classes.
    d. none of the above

2. Which of the following is most important when it comes to effective note taking?
    a. Taping the lecture
    b. Memorizing the recall column
    c. Identifying the main points
    d. Writing the information down verbatim

3. One method for organizing notes is called the
    a. Cornell format.   c. College success method.
    b. Jewler method.   d. none of the above

4. Syllabi are
    a. formal statements of course expectations.
    b. requirements and procedures of the course.
    c. a and b
    d. none of the above

5. When a lecturer is disorganized, you should
    a. wait until you get home to figure it out.
    b. organize what she/he says into general and specific frameworks.
    c. not disturb him/her during office hours.
    d. all of the above

True/False

6. During lecture, it is best to use shorthand and write down everything the teacher says verbatim.

7. It is not necessary or important to take notes on class discussions.

8. You cannot assume that college instructors lecture on the same material covered in the course text.

9. Listening in class is like listening to a TV.

Short Answer

10. Name some methods of note taking other than outlining.

11. List some reasons why sharing notes can be a good practice.

12. List some reasons why sharing notes can be counterproductive.

Essay

13. Describe three strategies you can use to listen critically during a lecture. Explain the benefits of using them and why they will work.

14. Draw a diagram of the Cornell method of note taking and list the parts. Then, discuss the benefits of using a note-taking system.

15. Describe some things you can do prior to the start of a lecture to prepare for learning and remembering.

16. Give a brief description of the note-taking formats that the text recommends. Discuss your personal preference.

17. Describe the steps to follow when taking notes. Which one(s) do you need to work on the most and why?

Answer Key

1. b, p. 66
2. c, p. 67
3. a, p. 66
4. c, p. 68
5. b, p. 67

6. false, p. 67
7. false, p. 68
8. true, p. 66
9. false, p. 68

Web Resources

Why We Forget   sarc.sdes.ucf.edu/learningskills/WhyWeForgetTEXT.html
The University of Central Florida hosts this Web page, which lists seven common reasons for forgetting information as well as suggestions to overcome each one.

Cornell system   www.ucc.vt.edu/stdysk/cornell.html

Note taking   www.dartmouth.edu/~acskills/success/notes.html
This page also includes tips on recognizing important information as well as additional note-taking aids.

Listening skills   www.infoplease.com/homework/listeningskills1.html

Participating in Class   www.drlynnfriedman.com/classparticipation.html
Clinical psychologist Dr. Lynn Friedman offers her opinions as to why it's important to participate in class discussion as well as suggestions on how to prepare to participate.

Applied Research   courseweb.gse.upenn.edu/~abrahaml/methods/appliedresearch.htm
A University of Pennsylvania master's degree candidate conducted applied research on "How Can I Create a Space for Less Vocal Students to Participate in Science Class?" The above link takes you to the index for the site, which goes through the methodology behind the project as well as the results.

For More Information

DePorter, B. and Hernacki, M. (2000). *Quantum notes: Whole brain approaches to note-taking.* Oceanside, CA: Learning Forum.

Helgesen, M. et al. (1995). *Active listening: Introducing skills for understanding (student's book 1).* New York: Cambridge University Press.

Kesselman-Turkel, J. and Peterson, F. (2003). *Note-taking made easy.* Madison, WI: University of Wisconsin Press.

Stanley, C. A. (2002). *Engaging large classes: Strategies and techniques for college faculty.* Bolton, MA: Anker Pub Co.

Winter, A. and Winter, R. (1997). *Brain workout: Easy ways to power up your memory, sensory perception, and intelligence.* New York: St. Martin's Press.

7 Reading for Success
Mastering an Essential Skill

Chapter Objectives

1. To explain how to prepare to read textbooks
2. To learn how to preview reading material
3. To learn how to read textbooks effectively
4. To learn how to mark textbooks
5. To learn how to review reading
6. To learn how to adjust your reading style to different types of books—quantitative, social sciences, and humanities
7. To facilitate vocabulary development

Timing of Chapter Coverage

Students will be given reading assignments during the first week of class. Many of these assignments will involve textbook reading because many of their first-term classes will be introductory (survey) courses. Your students may start to become inundated with the amount of textbook reading that is expected of them. It is particularly important that this chapter be covered in time to allow students to begin learning the required textbook material so they can adequately prepare for their first college exams.

About This Chapter

One of the most difficult aspects of the transition from learning in high school to mastering course work in college is developing strategies for reading different types of textbooks. In the beginning, first-year students tend to allocate too little time to adequately comprehend and retain textbook material. They may also be overly dependent on highlighting or underlining without understanding the role of other strategies that are used when reviewing for exams. Whatever method students choose, they should keep in mind that their ultimate purpose is to be able to read actively and critically while determining what is important and creating a system for review.

Since reading in college is more challenging to students, help them focus on the strategies in this chapter that will improve their reading skills. Explain to students that they will need to know that the amount and type of reading may change from what they have been used to, and they will also have to change their approach to textbook reading. For example, a textbook may be used as the main body of information in a course that will be included on exams. Let's face it, students will have to be able to actively read and learn this material if they are going to be successful.

This chapter offers solid strategies for working with textbook material. Encourage the development of a reading strategy and the use of the many skills included in the text such as mapping, monitoring comprehension, awareness of reading rate, and developing vocabulary. It is a good idea to help students practice these skills through in-class exercises and out-of-class assignments.

Depending on your students' needs, work with them to practice the strategies, identify their difficulties, and determine techniques that will help them improve their reading skills. Reading is critical to success in college. By helping your students develop these important reading strategies, they will begin to master textbook reading.

Suggested Outline for Addressing Topics in Chapter 7

Step 1   Begin with a lecture launcher or icebreaker activity

Step 2   Employ a variety of classroom activities

a. Use the PowerPoint presentation
b. Expand on key lesson themes
c. Involve students in a group activity
d. Involve peer leaders
e. Engage students in learning through case studies

Step 3   Review

a. Address common questions and concerns about the topic
b. Writing reflection

Expanded Lesson Plan

Step 1   Lecture Launchers and Icebreakers

- Demonstrating the practice of previewing is a good way to begin a discussion about the material in this chapter. Ask students to take out the textbook and look at the first page of a chapter they haven't been assigned to read as yet (perhaps the next chapter you plan to teach). Have one student read the title of the chapter. Ask your students what they already know about this subject. Next, ask them to read through the introductory paragraphs, the chapter headings, and subheadings. Remind them to note any study exercises at the end of the chapter. Now ask your students why taking these steps and the subsequent recommended previewing activities are important to their reading comprehension. Have students discuss how they normally read a chapter, and ask if they can see any differences between their usual method and the previewing one.

Step 2   Classroom Activities

a.   *Use the PowerPoint presentations to complement your mini-lecture.*

b.   *Key Lesson Themes*

COMPARING READING STRATEGIES

This activity is designed to facilitate learning across the curriculum and to encourage students to apply reading strategies in all their courses.

1.   Ask students to make copies of one chapter from each text used in three other courses they are currently taking.
2.   Have them highlight one chapter, annotate one, and take notes on the third.
3.   Ask students to do a writing assignment in which they evaluate which method assisted them most in retaining the chapter information and preparing for exams. Have them write about the pros and cons of each method.
4.   This approach should be meaningful to students because they are in essence studying for their other courses while completing your assignment.

VOCABULARY BUILDING

The following exercise is designed to illustrate that increasing one's vocabulary is an important part of the college reading process.

1.   Place students into groups of four. Tell them they are going to create a new vocabulary list of ten words and definitions.
2.   Have each group member use this and other textbooks to create the list. It may be mostly subject-specific vocabulary they come up with, but that is okay.
3.   If you can provide them with flip chart paper and markers, have them write out their lists. Members of each group can then present their list to the class.

c.   *Group Activities*

This exercise provides good practice for students. If time permits in class, give students a brief reading assignment from this text. Then ask them to process this exercise in pairs or small groups. Have them compare how they did as well as whether or not their notes contain the same main ideas. Processing this exercise with the class and pointing out the main ideas will be useful for many students.

d.   *Peer Leader Assistance*

•   In American culture we often talk about whether or not someone likes to read. A good way to start this chapter might be to have a brief discussion with your students about their reading interests. Ask them to share if they like to read, what they like to read (novels, magazines, newspapers), and when they read. This will give you some insight into their thoughts about reading. You should also let the students know your reading material style and preferences.

e.   *Case Studies*

SHONDRA

Shondra tells you that whenever she sits down to read her biology text she loses concentration or falls asleep. To her, it is *so boring.* Even when she does get through an entire chapter, she has no idea what she read. There is a lot of material included in each chapter. There are 25 chapters in this textbook that will be covered during the semester. The professor expects the class to read the textbook as well as take lecture notes. Both sets of information will be included on five tests they will have to take during the semester. Shondra has no idea how she will read all of the chapters, let alone how she will learn all the material. This class is a degree requirement for Shondra and one of four classes she is taking.

Discussion Questions

1.   What are Shondra's major issues concerning this class and her reading?
2.   What are Shondra's options?
3.   What suggestions would you make to assist Shondra?
4.   What kind of strategies could help Shondra?
5.   What other factors should be considered besides how she approaches her reading?

BARRY

Barry is taking a philosophy course. The instructor has asked the class to do some research on the Internet to find three Web sites that give information about any of the philosophers they have discussed so far. Each student will bring up one Web site on the classroom computer and tell the class some new information they have learned. The instructor tells students that the Web sites must be credible and have accurate information. Barry has never done any research on the Internet. He doesn't know how to begin. This assignment is due in the next class.

Discussion Questions

1.   How would you suggest Barry get started?
2.   What criteria could Barry use to evaluate the information on the Web sites he identifies?
3.   How can Barry get more practice in doing research on the Internet?
4.   What would alert Barry to the fact that a Web site may not be credible?
5.   How would Barry cite these Web sites in a paper?

Step 3   Review

a.   *Address Common Questions and Concerns of First-Year Students*

- *Why is there so much reading in college?*

  Answer: College takes a different approach to learning than many high school classes. As discussed in Chapter 4, students will need to be actively involved in their learning. This often means a lot of self-directed learning. Some instructors expect students to read a large amount of textbook material or even a wide range of articles and other materials outside of class. Help students grasp that they do not need to be frightened of these expectations and to understand that they can meet the challenge.

- *How can this reading method save me time? It looks like it takes more time.*

  Answer: Many students read their textbooks only to realize they have forgotten what they have read. Then they are still left to gather important textbook information to prepare for an exam. This method does take time and effort on the student's part; however, its benefits outweigh the time factor. Tell students this reading method will give them a greater understanding of the material, increase their ability to focus and concentrate, and produce materials that will help them study for tests and quizzes.

- *Wouldn't it be easier just to take a speed-reading course?*

  Answer: While speed-reading can be helpful to increase reading rate and comprehension, there are many other considerations for reading a textbook. Tell your students that someone who speed-reads still needs to organize the material for later review and exams.

- *Why should I read the text if the instructor is going to lecture on it?*

  Answer: Students need to evaluate how closely the lecture and textbook materials coincide. Warn students not to skip classes even if the lecture seems to follow the text exactly. Explain to them they will miss other learning opportunities that take place in the classroom and may become disconnected from their instructor or classmates.

- *Why should I bother to take notes on my reading? I can always read the chapters again before the test.*

  Answer: Many students think they can read the chapters again before a test. In reality, the time constraints of college and the large amount of material to study for a test often prohibit this practice. Remind students that they must balance the work in one class with the work in their other classes as well as outside commitments and responsibilities.

b.   *Writing Reflection*

- Leave a few minutes at the end of class for students to complete the Portfolio exercise on pages 86–87.

Test Questions

Multiple Choice

Choose ONE answer per question.

1. The first thing you should read when previewing a reading assignment is the
   a. chapter title.
   b. chapter outline.
   c. chapter summary.
   d. chapter assignments.

2. Developing a visual guide to a chapter is known as
   a. illustrating.
   b. chunking.
   c. mapping.
   d. outlining.

3. Dividing terms on a list into groups of five, seven, or nine is known as
   a. illustrating.
   b. chunking.
   c. mapping.
   d. outlining.

4. In most sciences, it is best to
   a. outline chapters.
   b. memorize lectures.
   c. tape record lectures.
   d. highlight the textbook as you read through it.

5. _____ is an example of a social science course.
   a. Biology
   b. Public Speaking
   c. History
   d. Calculus

6. _____ is an example of a humanities course.
   a. Biology
   b. Astronomy
   c. Literature
   d. Calculus

7. The final step in effective textbook reading is
   a. highlighting.
   b. reviewing.
   c. book marking.
   d. to copy it in your own handwriting.

True/False

8. To annotate is to use direct quotes.

9. You should mark your textbook as you skim it.

10. If you do not know a word in your reading, chances are it is unimportant.

Short Answer

11. List two common problems students have with textbooks

12. Describe the steps for effective textbook reading.

13. Name three basic vocabulary strategies mentioned in the chapter.

Essay

14. Do you think you will benefit most from highlighting, annotating, or outlining your text(s)? Why? Does it depend on the style of textbook or the subject matter? What other strategies do you intend to use to enhance comprehension and retention?

15. Describe some effective strategies for previewing chapters. Have you tried any of the methods presented in your text? If so, have they helped you read more efficiently? If not, which strategies do work for you?

Answer Key

1. a, p. 78
2. c, p. 78
3. b, p. 78
4. a, p. 83
5. c, p. 84

6. c, p. 84
7. b, p. 80
8. false, p. 78
9. false, p. 80
10. false, p. 81

Web Resources

How to Read www.ocean.edu/ReadColText/HowToReadCollegeTextDrJohnWeber.htm
Prepared by English professor Dr. John Weber, this site goes through the steps of proper college textbook reading, starting with previewing and finishing with a reminder that reading is an active process.

Concept Maps www.psywww.com/mtsite/mindmaps.html
Mind Tools offers this feature, which explains how concept mapping improves note taking and reading comprehension. It includes sample maps, tips for improving mapping skills, and a link to concept mapping software, which can be downloaded for a free, twenty-one-day trial.

Annotating Text www.bucks.edu/~specpop/Access/annotating.htm
Most students don't know how to highlight effectively. This site suggests annotating texts instead of simply highlighting them. It not only explains the best way to annotate information, but it also offers a link to an example of a well-annotated passage.

A Word A Day www.wordsmith.org/awad/
To encourage students to work on their vocabulary building skills, think about requiring them to register for the free version of this site. Each day they'll be e-mailed a new vocabulary word and its definition. You can monitor their comprehension of these words by giving weekly quizzes.

Inventory www.dvc.edu/english/Learning_Resources/TextbookReadingInventory.htm
Print out this textbook reading inventory and give it to your students. Ask them to fill it out for one (or several) reading assignments to demonstrate how the reading methods proposed in this chapter really do increase comprehension.

For More Information

Elder, J. (2003). *Exercise your college reading skills: Developing more powerful comprehension.* New York: McGraw Hill Humanities.

Langan, J. (1998). *Ten steps to advancing college reading skills* (3rd ed). West Berlin, NJ: Townsend Press.

Nist, S. L. and Mohr, C. (2002). *Advancing vocabulary skills* (3rd ed). West Berlin, NJ: Townsend Press.

Silvey, D. (2002). *Reading from the inside out: Increasing your comprehension and enjoyment of college reading.* New York: Longman.

Wintner, G. (1995). *Practical college reading: Strategies for comprehension and vocabulary.* Burr Ridge, IL: Irwin Professional Publishing.

8 Taking Exams and Tests
Putting All Your Essential Skills to the Test

Chapter Objectives

1. To help students prepare their minds and bodies for taking exams
2. To explore in what ways study groups and tutors can help students get ready for exams
3. To discuss how students can prepare for the special demands of exams in math and science
4. To explain how using sound study techniques and tools throughout the academic term can increase students' readiness for exams
5. To help students understand what steps to take to improve their skill in remembering
6. To provide students with tips to reduce test anxiety
7. To discuss what strategies students can apply to do their best on tests
8. To discuss how to answer different types of test questions

Timing of Chapter Coverage

Test taking is a critical skill that students will need to master. They may encounter differences in testing from what they were used to in high school. This chapter should be taught as soon as possible after you've addressed study skills and definitely before the first round of major exams occur.

About This Chapter

First-year students often have unrealistic expectations. Each student is different. While some strategies are more effective for certain students, there will always be some students who will be successful with what appears to be relatively little effort in some subjects. Other students will follow all the suggestions in this book and still be disappointed with their grades. These students need to learn from their test experiences in order to be better prepared in the future.

Students who use the methods suggested in the previous chapters are likely to be successful on exams. It is imperative that students understand that studying for exams begins on the first day of class. Encouraging students to form study groups can add to their success. A well-chosen study group provides students with the opportunity to assess their understanding of the material. Group discussions confirm or deny understanding. The study group also provides an opportunity to fill in any blanks that may exist through either misunderstanding, oversight, or absence. Also, different students will bring different approaches to studying, which can create a desirable richness to the group. Finally, the will of the group to study can overcome individual procrastination.

If you time the coverage of this chapter carefully, you will be able to discuss test preparation at about the time your first-year students are preparing to take their first major exams. This is also a good time to talk about test anxiety; unfortunately some students are not able to demonstrate their knowledge on exams because they fall prey to their fears about testing. Encourage those students who struggle with test anxiety to seek help to change this. For some of them, improving their study tools and memory strategies will help with some of the anxiety. Talking with instructors, tutors, and classmates can also be helpful. In cases like this, developing a positive relationship with faculty can be so important to a student's success.

It will be important that you help students to see that test preparation is a culmination of their ongoing study habits. Encourage them to develop a study system with both test taking and learning as the main objectives. Through the chapter information and exercises, have your students explore their past study strategies that lead up to exams and look for ways to make improvements on that.

Suggested Outline for Addressing Topics in Chapter 8

Step 1   Begin with a lecture launcher or icebreaker activity

Step 2   Employ a variety of classroom activities

    a. Use the PowerPoint presentation
    b. Expand on key lesson themes
    c. Involve students in a group activity
    d. Involve peer leaders
    e. Engage students in learning through case studies

Step 3   Review

    a. Address common questions and concerns about the topic
    b. Writing reflection

Expanded Lesson Plan

Step 1   Lecture Launchers and Icebreakers

- You may find that your students' expectations of college tests and exams are somewhat different than those in high school. Begin by asking students to discuss the differences they are encountering in different class tests. They may note such things as types of exams, amount of material on each exam, and deciding on what to study for an exam. Having this discussion with students will help them to identify these differences and allow them to determine how they will make adjustments in exam preparation.

Step 2   Classroom Activities

    a. Use the PowerPoint presentations to complement your mini-lecture.

    b. Key Lesson Themes

ESSAY EXAMS

Use this activity to show students a method of planning for essay-based exams and to give students practice on how to prepare for essay test questions:

1. Using the list of key task words in the chapter, ask groups to prepare six or seven potential essay questions from their notes.

2. Have each student choose one of the questions and prepare a brief outline to share with the other students.
3. Next, ask students to critique each other's outlines.
4. Bring in concrete essay questions illustrating the different key task words. Do not assume that students will understand them without examples.

EXAM QUESTIONS

Use this activity to give students practice preparing for other types of exam questions.
1. Use the test construction strategy similar to the one suggested for essay (above).
2. Ask each student to construct ten objective questions for a chapter of this text.
3. Then, test the students using the questions they have constructed.

TEST ANXIETY

Invite a counselor or student affairs professional to share their expertise and provide practical ways to control or overcome test anxiety.

c. *Group Activities*
   - Ask students to brainstorm pros and cons about study groups. Have the groups report back, and ask the class to offer suggestions on how to change the cons into pros.

d. *Peer Leader Assistance*
   - You can share your personal experiences with test anxieties. What memories do you have with high stake tests: ACT, SAT, GRE?
   - Spend some time addressing the importance of preparing physically for a test.

e. *Case Studies*

CHRISTOPHER

Christopher asks to talk to his professor about the results of his first exam in his American History class. Christopher is a pre-law major, and his success in this course is very important to him. He tells the professor that he loves history and always earned the highest grades in his history classes in high school. Christopher has always used the reading, note-taking, and test-preparation strategies he learned in class, and thought he was well prepared for the history exam. However, he acknowledges that he guessed at many of the items on the multiple-choice part of the exam. He thought he had done well on the essay, but he scored only 30 out of the 50 possible points. Overall, Christopher received a grade of 63 out of 100 points.

Discussion Questions
1. How would you respond to Christopher?
2. What could have gone wrong with Christopher's test preparation?
3. What could have gone wrong during the exam?
4. What suggestions do you have for Christopher?
5. What exam preparation system would you suggest that Christopher utilize for his next exam?

AN-YI

An-Yi is getting close to the deadline for her ten-page term paper in her environmental studies class. She has had eight weeks to research and write the paper and now she finds herself with another three days left before it is due. She finds the class boring and doesn't see how it relates to her major, business. An-Yi got her topic approved by her instructor during the first week as required, but she hasn't done a thing since then. She is panicking, but she still doesn't have the motivation to write the paper. One of An-Yi's close friends suggests a Web site where you can purchase research papers on any topic. She tells An-Yi to buy one and modify it a little to make it her own work. An-Yi is seriously considering doing this.

Discussion Questions
1. What are An-Yi's important issues here?
2. What suggestions do you have for An-Yi?
3. What alternatives does An-Yi have?
4. If An-Yi purchases and modifies a paper, would this be considered cheating?
5. What consequences would An-Yi face if this is considered cheating?

Step 3   Review

a.   *Address Common Questions and Concerns of First-Year Students*

- *How do I know what kind of questions the teacher will ask on the test?*

  Answer: Some instructors are very clear about the types of questions that will be on a test. Others are not. Students will have to listen carefully in the classroom for this information. If the instructor is not specific, they can talk with the instructor after class or during office hours as well as consult their classmates for additional insight.

- *How can I be sure I am studying the right things?*

  Answer: Again, some instructors will be very clear about the material a particular test will cover, while others may not. Students may find that some instructors give a review before a test and may even hand out a study outline. Checking with reliable classmates may often help students if they are unsure. Emphasize to students that being actively involved in their own learning will help with knowing what to study for a test.

- *Why not pull an all-nighter? I always do better under pressure.*

  Answer: Cutting back on sleep is not a good idea because it deprives the brain of the rest it needs to work at full power. Students need sleep to do their best critical thinking and remain alert during exams. Encourage students to maintain their regular sleep routines before exams.

- *How will I ever learn six weeks' worth of information in time to pass this test?*

  Answer: Preparing for exams should actually start on the first day of the term. Lecture notes, reading information, and doing homework are all part of the preparation. Explain to students that organizing course materials and good time management will aid their learning and are best if done right from the start of class, not one week or a few days before a test. Studying and organizing material right before a test may be too late to learn all the material and perform well on the test.

- *Is it okay to work together on a take-home math exam? In class the teacher always has us solve problems in small groups.*

  Answer: Unless specifically told that it is okay to collaborate, this is usually not acceptable. Even with take-home exams, instructors still expect that students will do their own work and are looking to evaluate them on just that. When in doubt, tell students to check with the instructor.

b.   *Writing Reflection*

- Ask students to write about their reactions to the material that was covered in this chapter.

Test Questions

Multiple Choice

Choose ONE answer per question.

1. What step can you take to prepare for tests?
    a. Ask your instructor about the exam.
    b. Manage your time wisely.
    c. Sharpen your study habits.
    d. all of the above

2. A mind map is essentially a
    a. review sheet
    b. brain scanner
    c. a and b
    d. none of the above

3. A design for test preparation is commonly referred to as a(n)
    a. mind map.
    b. review sheet.
    c. flashcard.
    d. exam plan.

4. After reading a multiple-choice question, the best way to answer is to
    a. first predict the answer, then pick a choice that matches your thought.
    b. assume that the letter of the correct answer is different from the previous question.
    c. read the choices at least three times.
    d. eliminate choices that you do not understand.

5. Answer choices that contain words like *always, never,* and *only* are
    a. often correct.
    b. always correct.
    c. often incorrect.
    d. always incorrect.

6. The technique of using self-messages that are encouraging rather than stress-provoking is called
    a. review sheet.
    b. acing a test.
    c. cognitive restructuring.
    d. none of the above

7. Instructors tend to prefer essay exams because they promote
    a. mind maps.
    b. memorization.
    c. higher-order critical thinking.
    d. none of the above

True/False

8. According to the text, attempting to study in front of the TV is likely to be a waste of your study time.

9. Always respond *True* to a true/false question that contains the word *always.*

Short Answer

10. Give two tips for successful test taking.

11. Give three tips for answering essay questions.

Essay Questions

12. Your final exam in sociology will be all essay questions. You will have three hours to respond to your choice of six essays out of ten options provided. List and describe the steps for your strategy for completing this exam.

13. Describe how and why doing well on exams can depend on physical and emotional preparation.

14. Give advice to a student who is flunking her exams because of test anxieties. Help this student understand the sources, identify the symptoms, and offer strategies for combating test anxieties.

15. Now that you have studied this chapter on test taking, what have you identified as keeping you from performing at your peak level academically? What changes do you propose to make? What are some of the outcomes you envision you'll receive from making these changes?

Answer Key

1. d, p. 90
2. a, p. 92
3. d, p. 93
4. a, p. 97
5. c, p. 97

6. c, p. 91
7. c, p. 97
8. true, p. 95
9. false, p. 97

Web Resources

Test taking strategies   www.mtsu.edu/~studskl/teststrat.html

www.eop.mu.edu/study/

Taking Multiple-Choice Tests   core.ecu.edu/psyc/wuenschk/TestTips.htm
More test taking tips can be found on this page, which focuses on how to improve success when facing multiple-choice questions.

For More Information

Buzan, T. (2003). *How to mind map: Make the most of your mind and learn to create, organize, and plan.* New York: Thorsons Pub.

Educational Testing Service. (2004). *Reducing test anxiety (Praxis study guides).* Princeton, NJ: Author.

Myers, J. N. (2000). *The secrets of taking any test* (2nd ed). San Diego, CA: Learning Express, Inc.

Robinson, Adam. (1993). *What smart students know: Maximum grades, optimum learning, minimum time.* New York: Three Rivers Press.

Rozakis, L. (2002). *Test taking strategies and study skills for the utterly confused.* New York: McGraw-Hill Trade.

9 Relationships, Diversity, and Values
Understanding and Respecting Yourself and Others

Chapter Objectives

1. To explore why and how students' various personal relationships are important to their success in college
2. To determine individually whether a serious relationship is right for students
3. To recognize and deal with intimate-partner violence in a relationship
4. To explore in ways relationships with parents or family members change when students are attending college
5. To help students understand what diversity and multicultural education mean in a college setting
6. To discuss what are the appropriate and the most personally beneficial ways to approach campus diversity
7. To explore what we mean by "values"
8. To learn to distinguish between means values and ends values

Timing of Chapter Coverage

You may teach this chapter at any time during the term. It is probably best to give your students a chance to become acquainted with one another before discussing a topic as sensitive as this one.

About This Chapter

If you read student journals over the course of the semester, you will find them dealing again and again with relationships—sometimes with pleasure, but sometimes with significant frustration or pain. Students may seem remarkably shortsighted or unperceptive in dealing with their relationships. What may seem entirely obvious to you may literally not even have occurred to them. Don't hesitate to write comments to your students when this happens. Students rarely resent this, and most appreciate your concern, even if they don't take your advice. Students are deeply grateful for your role as a confidant and your feedback and attention to their social dilemmas. Learning to deal constructively with relationships is a genuinely educational part of entering students' experience. You may be sure that your facilitation of their understanding and maturing in relationships will be an appropriate and welcome part of their college education.

Teaching issues of diversity in any American classroom is very challenging. The trick is to teach the material in such a manner that the emotions become a part of the intellectual understanding students will develop. This is not easy and will require you to be in touch with your own emotions as you deal with this topic. An emphasis on social change is critical. Students will benefit more if they come to an understanding that what they know, what they learn, and what they believe will be challenged by changes in all of the variables. It is the ability to recognize change and handle it in an appropriate manner that will be a major indicator of a well-educated person.

The topic of moral values has been politicized: there is pressure on first-year students to adopt the "right" moral values. One of the books in the bibliography makes this point, but it does so in a manner that can be very helpful as a teaching tool: *American Values: Opposing Viewpoints.* There are six chapter topics for this book, all with spirited excerpts:

1. What values should America uphold?

2. How are American values changing?

3. Is America in decline? (with specific readings by William Bennett "Moral Conduct is in Decline" and "Moral Conduct is Not in Decline" by Jeffrey W. Hayes and Seymour Martin Lipset)

4. How important are family values?

5. How do religious values influence America?

6. How does materialism affect America?

The point is that there are rich resources in the arena of moral values for stimulating assignments using the Web or examples from current events in the newspaper.

Suggested Outline for Addressing Topics in Chapter 9

Step 1   Begin with a lecture launcher or icebreaker activity

Step 2   Employ a variety of classroom activities

  a. Use the PowerPoint presentation
  b. Expand on key lesson themes
  c. Involve students in a group activity
  d. Involve peer leaders
  e. Engage students in learning through case studies

Step 3   Review

  a. Address common questions and concerns about the topic
  b. Writing reflection

Expanded Lesson Plan

Step 1   Lecture Launchers and Icebreakers

  • Consider each of the following "axioms of relationships" that are suggested. Are they true? If so, how can they be used to avoid bad relationships and build good ones? If you like, have your students form gender-mixed groups and discuss each axiom. Then they can report back to the class. This is sure to start off the chapter in a lively manner.
    • If it is the right relationship, it will work; if it doesn't work, it isn't the right relationship.
    • Every bad relationship has warning signs.
    • Having no relationship is better than having a bad relationship.
    • Don't settle for less than you deserve.
    • Get it right the first time—divorce is hell.
    • You will have the best relationship when you don't need one. That is, when you are content with your own life, you won't be searching for a relationship to fill a gap.
    • When it comes to partners in relationships, it is better for the other person to want you more than need you, and it is better to want rather than need the other person.

Step 2   Classroom Activities

a.   *Use the PowerPoint presentations to complement your mini-lecture.*

b.   *Key Teaching Themes*

The exercises that follow are challenging. Some are more challenging than others. They are designed to push students beyond their perceived limits and lead them into deeper and more compelling learning experiences.

1. Every American comes to understand that people are treated differently based on their skin complexion. Have your students write a brief essay describing their memory of when they first realized people are treated differently because of their complexion. Ask them to describe what that experience meant to them, or you could generate a classroom discussion on this topic.

2. Based on the data from the 2000 census of the American population, have your students analyze the racial and ethnic composition of their hometown, county, and state. They can do this by going to **www.census.gov/** and selecting American Fact Finder. They can then follow the prompts to locate their home state, county, and city. Have them review the year 2000 data for each unit and write an essay on the racial and ethnic composition of each unit, making sure they discuss its significance in their lives. If possible, ask them to find similar data for the 1990 census and compare the two periods of time.

c.   *Group Activities*

TAKE A VALUE STAND

This exercise is designed to help students learn how to disagree, or agree to disagree, and to show students how to open their minds to an opposing point of view.

Suggestions

1. The time required is about one hour. The setting required is an open room that is large enough to hold the class (unobstructed by tables and chairs). The instructor uses masking tape on the floor (or posts signs on three of the walls) to designate areas for students to stand if they Agree (A), are Uncertain/Unclear(U), or Disagree (D).

2. Participants may stand anywhere in the beginning. Ask them to move towards the areas designated as **A**, **U**, or **D** in response to the statements that the facilitator will read. They have no option but to take a stand. If they are uncertain, they may stand in the center, but in doing so, they are committing themselves to explain why. Several issues are grouped, and discussion doesn't need to take place until the entire group of issues is read. For example, read all of statement #1's lines before asking for feedback, and ask participants to change their positions as the statement is altered. At this point the facilitator will ask the participants to sit and will request that students explain their point-of-view.

3. Because of time, choose only those statements that are relevant to the demographics of the class. You may want to add some new ones that include current events and news headlines.

4. After a statement is read, give students 30–45 seconds to decide which section best fits their response. The leader can then give the signal for everyone to move to the section they chose. This encourages students to think on their own and minimizes peer pressure ("Where are my friends standing?").

5. Remember, this is not a debate exercise! Some students will be tempted to give a feedback rebuttal after someone has expressed an opinion different than their own. Try to avoid this. A good way of avoiding a rebuttal–debate is by allowing a person to speak only once per issue.

6. Some people are quieter than others and vice versa. The more vocal people tend to always voice their opinions. While this is the way most classes run, it is imperative that in "Take a Value Stand," the more quiet students get their opinions heard. To encourage this, try saying, "Let's hear from someone we haven't heard from yet." This usually works like a charm. If it doesn't, pick someone.

7. With people who haven't been in a situation where their views are directly challenged, there is a tendency to avoid making decisions. As a result, a group of people may insist on sitting in the Uncertain/Undecided area. A good trick is to make it a rule that all those who chose to stand in the middle MUST voice their opinions. In doing this, the quiet ones that chose to stand there know they will be picked on and will prepare themselves.

8. "Take a Value Stand" is about differences, and history has shown us that differences and the ignorance of the "other" are what people fear the most. Because of this, opinions are sometimes met with tension and friction, especially when people begin to make whispered comments while others are talking or make shocked remarks at someone's opinion. How you handle this is up to you, but it is imperative that you deal with it. Be prepared for it to come up.

9. Different people define the statements differently. Try to avoid defining it for them. For example, in the statement, "Women make good secretaries on committees," avoid defining whether you mean "only women" or "all women" or "women but not men." Let students work it out.

The Statements

1. I believe in the commandment, "Thou shalt not kill."
   — I would *not* kill in defense of my country.
   — I would *not* kill in defense of my family.
   — I would *not* kill in defense of my own life.

2. I do not believe in euthanasia (mercy killing). I would not pull the plug on the machine keeping my great grandmother of 96 years of age alive if she had a terminal disease and was in pain even if
   — she asked me to.
   — she asked me to three times.
   — she asked me to every time I visited her.

3. When a friend is doing something illegal or dangerous to himself or herself and it makes me feel uncomfortable, I would
   — shrug it off and do nothing.
   — joke about it.
   — ask him or her to stop.
   — get mad at him or her.
   — just leave.

4. I believe that athletes who have contracted HIV/AIDS should be barred from playing contact sports.
5. If I were assigned a roommate who was HIV-positive, I would ask for a roommate change.
6. I believe that women should be permitted
   — to serve in the military.
   — to serve as pilots, naval officers, and support staff to front-line roles.
   — to serve in combat roles.
7. I believe that gays and lesbians should be permitted to serve openly in the armed services.
8. I believe that if a long-time close friend confided in me that she or he was homosexual, it would not affect our friendship.
9. It is okay with my parents for people of different races (including you) to
   — date occasionally.
   — have a steady relationship.
   — get married.
10. When it comes to relationships, the opposite sex thinks only about sex.
11. For women, money is an extremely important thing when they are looking for a relationship.
12. Birth control is the woman's responsibility.
13. It is okay for a woman to initiate sexual activity during a date. A woman can be bold and up front about her sexual needs.
14. Initially, I am attracted to someone because of his or her personality.
15. I would date someone who had a terrific personality but who was obese.
16. It is okay and appropriate for a woman to call a man for a date.
17. I would date someone who has a terrific personality but is physically disabled.
18. Women who initiate a dating relationship tend to be overbearing.
19. After a break-up, the two people involved can remain friends.
20. Women are more sensitive than men.
21. Single parents should be able to adopt.
22. Homosexuality is wrong.
23. Gay couples should be permitted to adopt children.
24. Women should have the ultimate decision-making responsibility with respect to whether to have the child or have an abortion.
25. Sex before marriage is wrong.
26. It is okay and in fact expected that men will sleep around.
27. A woman who sleeps with two different men is sleazy.
28. I believe in not using racial slurs.
29. I see nothing wrong with telling or laughing at ethnic jokes.
30. A person's religion is his or her own business, and a person is free to believe whatever he or she wants as long as it does not infringe on other people's rights.
31. I would date people who are of a different religion than I am.
32. We are all created equal. The color of a person's skin should not affect how people are treated.
33. When I come in contact with a large number of people from a different ethnic group, I become anxious.
34. When I hear the word *gang,* I usually associate it with ethnic groups.
35. When I hear the term *terrorist,* I usually associate it with Middle Easterners.
36. Bilingual education should be eliminated from public schools.
37. Able-bodied students should be given prior notice if their roommate is disabled.

38. It is harder to relate to someone who is physically disabled than to someone who is not.
39. Disabled students should have special priority for admission to college.
40. I would not have a problem if my R.A.
    — was hearing impaired.
    — was deaf.
    — had a learning disability.
    — had cerebral palsy.
    — was mobility impaired.
41. Smoking dope should disqualify a candidate for consideration for a Supreme Court position or for the presidency of the United States.
42. I believe the California coast should be opened to oil drilling.
43. Voter ballots should be printed in languages other than English.
44. The legal drinking age in every state should be lowered to 18.
45. Flag burning should be illegal.
46. Grades are a fair indicator of
    — who I am as a person.
    — how much I learned in that class.
47. People who only belong to ethnic clubs or groups on campus limit themselves.
48. Affirmative action policies shouldn't have an effect on college admissions.
49. Students who are caught plagiarizing should be expelled, no questions asked.
50. Students should be allowed to date their professors.

DEBRIEFING THE "TAKE A VALUE STAND" EXERCISE

Suggestions

1. Debrief students in small groups or pairs.
2. Begin by asking for general feedback about the exercise.
3. Ask them the following specific questions:
   • Were there any surprises?
   • Did you find yourself making assumptions and stereotypes about a person on the other side before you heard what they had to say?
   • Is this exercise designed for you to learn more about other people or yourself?

d. Peer Leader Assistance

• Plan a field trip to the cafeteria or food court. Have students analyze patterns of social affiliation during the lunchtime hours (usually 11:00 A.M. to 1:00 P.M.). Ask them to observe where people sit, with whom they sit, and their patterns of interaction. See if they can identify those sections of the cafeteria often occupied by different social groups (athletes, fraternities, sororities, commuters, international students, minority students, and others). Have them write an essay on at least two of these groups on the subject, "Why (group A) and (group B) always sit together for lunch."

e.   *Case Studies*

RENEE

Renee's English teacher stops her at the end of class and asks if they can set up a meeting. Naturally, Renee is a bit apprehensive; most student-teacher conferences seem to focus on problems. But when she arrives for the meeting, Renee is pleasantly surprised—at first. Her teacher says, "I just wanted to compliment you on your writing skills. You are doing beautifully in my class . . ." Renee is about to thank her teacher when she hears the next words: ". . . for an African American student." Renee is stunned and speechless. She doesn't know what to say. She gets up, turns, and walks out the door without saying anything. Her eyes become teary as she quickly moves toward the door of the building and heads for her next class.

Discussion Questions

1. Why do you think Renee's teacher would say something like that?
2. Was Renee overreacting to the statement? Explain your answer.
3. Did Renee do the right thing by walking out of the office without saying a word? What else could/should she have done to explain her feelings?
4. Was there a lesson for the teacher here? If so, what was it and how could Renee help her understand it?

PROFESSOR HARRIS, JAMES, CHRISTINA, AND TY

In a college success course, Professor Harris announces that two members of the Gay and Lesbian Student Association will be visiting class at the next meeting. One student, James, says, "What are they going to do, try and convert us?" Another, Christina, says, "It's against my religion." Ty chimes in, "I refuse to be in the same room with them." The other students simply sit there and stare at one another.

Discussion Questions

1. Should Professor Harris abort the plan to invite the students? Explain.
2. Should Professor Harris explain why it's important to invite the students? How would she justify this?
3. Apart from the statements made by James, Christina, and Ty, what do you think was going on in the minds of most students in this class when Professor Harris made the announcement? What would you say made them think or feel this way?
4. How would you react if you were in the class? Explain.

Step 3 Review

a. *Address Common Questions and Concerns of First-Year Students*

- *I'm afraid I'll say something that will offend someone of another race.*
  Answer: It will happen, and sometimes you may not even know it. Use common sense and work on building a relationship with someone you like. Don't go out of your way to be friendly with other minority students if you really have little in common with them. Ask yourself, "Would I be friends with this person if he or she were from the same culture as I am?"

- *I don't think I'm part of any cultural group.*
  Answer: Everyone is part of some cultural group. It might be interesting to ask members of your family where your ancestors came from. You may discover that, rather than being part of one group exclusively, you are actually a mixture of several.

- *Is it okay to refer to people by race?*
  Answer: People from different countries usually categorize themselves by their homelands not by race. Words such as "black" and "negro," used at various times in our history, have given way to the concept of "African-American," which more closely defines a group of people by its place of origin. As you well know, some "black" students are not very black at all, and the word *negro* is considered a demeaning term used in the last century and earlier.

- *Are students of one culture naturally smarter than students of another?*
  Answer: Not at all! You will find students of above-average intelligence in all cultural groups, just as you will find students who are average or below average. Because African-Americans were deprived for years of schooling comparable to their white counterparts, many thought they were not capable of learning. Few, if any, believe that today.

- *I get nervous when someone of my sex starts acting in a way that makes me think he or she is gay. I'm not gay and I don't want to be involved with gay people.*
  Answer. Gays and lesbians make up around 10% of the population, according to some estimates. So it's almost impossible to isolate yourself from this group. Gays and lesbians are the last group to "come out" and defend their right to enjoy all of the opportunities and privileges of the straight majority. Remember, most gays and lesbians won't be interested in you sexually. Are you madly in love with everyone of the opposite sex you meet?

- *Older students are threatening because they are more serious about their studies and "raise the bar" in classes they attend. How can I survive with them in my classes?*
  Answer: Think a moment about the added demands on older students that you don't have to concern yourself with: keeping house, earning a living, raising a family, caring for elders and children, and so forth. Sure, they're going to work hard; they've invested lots of time and energy into getting a college degree. Instead of feeling challenged by them, get to know them. You'll learn a lot.

- *Why is such an emphasis placed on societal values in this chapter?*
  Answer: The reason for this emphasis is that American society has changed dramatically over the past half-century, and changes in values have followed from those structural changes. Further, with the explosion of information technology and the effects of globalization, the pace of change will likely accelerate. The society as a whole and its basic institutions smuggle (try to impose in hidden or deceptive ways) values. Since those values are changing, it is even more difficult for students to define their most enduring values.

- *Why was the specific format for classifying values chosen for this chapter?*
  Answer: The first reason is that moral values are central to the fabric of civil society. There is no way that a humane society can be constructed based on law alone. Moral values are also the crucible for significant family relationships where there are such shared obligations for mutual welfare. Aesthetic and performance values are hallmarks of individual difference. The college years are a time when the very institution of higher education challenges students to expand their horizons on both types of values. Instrumental and Intrinsic value categories are very credible contributions from the science of value research to understanding the functions of values in people's lives. It is also possible to compare these values across generations, i.e. to understand the "generation gap." The vignette from actor Russell Crowe and his father emphasizes this gap.

b. *Writing Reflection*
Have students reflect upon what they learned about diversity in this chapter.

Test Questions

Multiple Choice

Choose ONE answer per question.

1. If it is time to end a relationship, do it
   a. immediately.
   b. sternly.
   c. calmly and cleanly.
   d. all of the above

2. Relationships ＿＿＿＿＿ when they turn into long-distance romances.
   a. flourish
   b. change significantly
   c. become problematic
   d. none of the above

3. Electronic relationships can be
   a. fun and educational.
   b. transient and unpredictable.
   c. a and b
   d. none of the above

4. ＿＿＿＿＿ are parts of culture.
   a. Traditions and foods
   b. Language and clothing styles
   c. Artistic expression and beliefs
   d. all of the above

5. Moral values
   a. justify our behavior toward others.
   b. should be imposed on others.
   c. are something everyone inherits from their parents.
   d. separate means from ends.

6. Aesthetic values
   a. justify our behavior toward others.
   b. apply to a broad set of judgments about beauty.
   c. refer to values on performing to a set standard.
   d. have a relationship to ethical standards.

7. Means values are to instrumental values as ends values are to
   a. performance values.
   b. external values.
   c. intrinsic values.
   d. societal values.

True/False

8. Latinos share the Spanish language.

9. Colleges and universities are protected from acts of discrimination and prejudice.

Short Answer

10. Give an example of a moral value, an aesthetic value, and a performance value.

11. What are two downsides of having a long-distance relationship?

12. List three ways in which colleges and universities can promote multiculturalism in higher education.

Essay

13. Do you believe colleges and universities should play an active role in educating students about diversity? Why or why not?

14. How does the information in this chapter differ from what you previously heard about race, culture, and ethnicity?

15. Write a community covenant or university creed that protects students from discrimination, prejudice, and insensitivity on your university campus. Develop a plan of action that could result in your university making this creed or covenant an institutional policy.

16. Write an essay on the one major lesson you learned from this chapter.

Answer Key

1. c, p. 103
2. b, p. 102
3. c, p. 105
4. d, p. 106
5. a, p. 108

6. b, p. 108
7. c, p. 109
8. true, p. 106
9. false, p. 107

Web Resources

Diversity Database   www.inform.umd.edu/EdRes/Topic/Diversity/
Maintained by the University of Maryland, this database contains links to everything from a "Diversity Dictionary" to issue-specific sources such as background information on various races and ethnicities.

Race and Campus Climate   www.diversityweb.org/Digest/Sm97/eloquently.html
Written by Mary K. Rouse, Dean of Students, and Roger Howard, Associate Dean of Students, at the University of Wisconsin–Madison, this essay explores the racial climate on their campus and how it has changed over time.

The Prejudice Institute   www.prejudiceinstitute.org/
The Prejudice Institute bills itself as "a resource for activists, lawyers, and social scientists . . . devoted to policy research and education on all dimensions of prejudice, discrimination, and ethnoviolence." It features free fact sheets about topics relating to prejudice as well as an article examining the sociopolitical conditions in America post-September 11.

Tolerance.org   www.tolerance.org/hidden_bias/
Created by psychologists at Harvard and the University of Washington, this site offers several tests that assess the "hidden" prejudices and biases we all have. Each test offers a tutorial that teaches users about the science behind the tests, stereotypes and prejudice, and the societal effects of bias.

Understanding Stereotypes   school.discovery.com/lessonplans/programs/stereotypes/
Although this lesson plan is geared toward high school students, it is easily adapted to the college classroom. The included Web links—historical timelines for various ethnic groups and several pages on tolerance—should prove useful as well.

How Race is Lived in America   www.nytimes.com/library/national/race/
This series of articles by the *New York Times* is based on the premise that race relations are being defined less by political action than by daily experience. It includes archival articles and a list of resources found on the Internet. Free registration is required.

More Helpful Links

sln.fi.edu/tfi/hotlists/blackhistory.html
Twenty-seven links to black history Web sites.

www.columbia.edu/cu/lweb/indiv/southasia/cuvl/
South Asia Resource Access provides links to Asian Interest Web sites

www.chcp.org/
Chinese historical and cultural project that promotes Chinese American culture

hirsch.cosy.sbg.ac.at/www-virtual-library_culture.html
Various links to different cultural Web sites

Personal Responsibility   www.heritage.org/Research/PoliticalPhilosophy/HL515.cfm
You can find this lecture on "The American Tradition of Personal Responsibility" on the Web site for The Heritage Foundation, a conservative organization. The essay, while pushing a specific agenda, raises several questions for your students to think about while learning the material from this chapter

For More Information

Bonilla-Silva, E. (2003). *Racism without racists: Color-blind racism and the persistence of racial inequality in the United States.* Lanham, MD: Rowman and Littlefield.

Caron, S. L. (2002). *Sex matters for college students: Sex FAQ's in human sexuality.* Upper Saddle River, NJ: Prentice Hall.

Griffin, J. H. (1996). *Black like me.* New York: Signet Classics.

Hollinger, D. A. (2000). *Postethnic America: Beyond multiculturalism.* New York: Basic Books.

Josephson, M. S. and Hanson, W., eds. (1998). *The power of character: Prominent Americans talk about life, family, work, values, and more.* San Francisco: Jossey-Bass.

Marcus, E. (1999). *Is it a choice?—revised edition: Answers to 300 of the most frequently asked questions about gays and lesbians.* San Francisco: Harper San Francisco.

Von Loewe Kreuter, G. (1996). *Forgotten promise: Race and gender wars on a small college campus.* New York: Knopf.

10 Staying Healthy
Managing Stress and Achieving Wellness

Chapter Objectives

1. To understand why managing stress is important
2. To discuss with students how they can manage stress by paying attention to their diets, exercise habits, sleep patterns, and relaxation needs
3. To discuss the many options students have for contraception and safer sex
4. To learn how to avoid getting a sexually transmitted infection (STI)
5. To discuss symptoms of STIs
6. To explore what we know about alcohol use and smoking among college students
7. To discuss the consequences of abusing prescription drugs and using illegal drugs

Timing of Chapter Coverage

This chapter introduces students to survival skills that help them do well in school. These skills are developed over time and with exposure to challenges. Students may benefit from being introduced to these skills early in the term, but the material could be covered at any time. You may consider reviewing the section on campus crime earlier than you do the rest of this chapter.

About This Chapter

Stress

It is helpful for the instructor to mention some typical aspects of college life that students find stressful. They will come to understand that the stressors they feel are common, and they are not alone in their struggle to handle them. The challenge is to get students to be introspective enough to recognize their own stress. Once this happens, strategies can be developed. Stress management is a personal behavior change. Research indicates that behavior change is very difficult for most people. Two elements seem to improve the rate of behavior change. First, people who develop an action plan with specific goals and specific actions that lead to the outcome seem to be more successful. Help the students to be specific with their action plans including active verbs, time frames, and evaluation. Second, people who incorporate the changes in their life plan are more successful with behavior change. Make sure the students understand that the way these pathways are established is through practice. Any behavior change when introduced into a life pattern seems awkward. It is not familiar and comfortable. But with practice it becomes normal. You could also encourage students to find a friend who is interested in behavior change and in teaming up to provide support for each other. For example, some students might want to initiate an aerobic exercise program. They could do this together and help each other stay committed to the plan. Some additional things to remember:

- Don't preach. Lead the students through discussion where they identify the important issues and questions.
- Set up a scavenger hunt and have students identify resources on campus that can help them with college stress. Do the same with resources for crime prevention.

- Teach students how to take their own pulse. They can use this information to determine if they are exercising aerobically.

- Demonstrate how exercise raises pulse rate by having the students take their pulse, do jumping jacks for three minutes, and then take their pulse again.

- Have students do an analysis of their diet, exercise, and caffeine intake.

- Record the relaxation technique in the book chapter and play it in class, play a professional tape, or have a counselor come to class and do one.

Sex

Chances are, students have been exposed to lectures on the basics of female and male anatomy, contraception, and STIs during their high school years. To present the material in this chapter, you do not have to be a "sex educator." You do, however, have to be comfortable talking to others in groups about sexuality. Establishing clear ground rules for class discussion may help diffuse discomfort. A good introductory class activity is to ask the class to brainstorm "rules" that will support a safe, non-threatening environment for everyone to participate. Examples of ground rules are:

- nothing that is said in class is to be repeated outside of class.

- Refrain from laughing at or criticizing others' opinions.

- Respect others' points of view.

- No talking while others are talking.

This activity can be conducted with the entire class as a large group or in pairs reporting back to the whole group. Visibly record the rules on the board and review them with the class. Ask a volunteer to copy the rules to notebook paper and then you can make copies and distribute them to the class at the next session. It may be helpful to refer students to the handout of "rules" before each class or on an as-needed basis.

One important reminder: As an instructor, your role in communicating key points from the chapter is not to judge, criticize, or moralize. While you may have strong personal beliefs about sex, your role is to present factual information, help students clarify their own values, and facilitate responsible sexual decision-making, whatever your students' viewpoints and choices may be.

If you feel that you are unable or are too uncomfortable to review the content in this chapter, that's okay. Rather than skip the chapter altogether, however, you may wish to access campus and community resources. Many colleges and universities have student health and wellness centers with trained staff whose responsibilities include speaking to classes, counseling students, working with faculty and staff, and preparing sex education materials. Ask colleagues or consult your campus and community phone directories for assistance in locating speakers and supplemental materials.

One of the challenges of teaching topics like sex that can stir emotions and trigger conflicting values is knowing *how* to respond to student questions. When a student asks or makes an awkward, embarrassing, or personal question or statement, *how* you answer is as important as *what* you answer. The following tips may help you:

- **Legitimize the question or statement.** Let the student know you have heard and understood: "That's a good question; lots of people ask/think/feel that."

- **React positively.** No matter how shocking, unusual, or revealing the question or statement, the student needs to know you won't reject him/her. Look the student in the eye and smile: "I'm glad you asked/said that. I know it must be difficult to talk about this."

- **Be careful of your own negative feelings.** Don't let your own feelings interfere; a negative or fearful response will cut off communication. Keep your body language relaxed and avoid "put downs" (e.g., "You're too young to . . .", "Where did you ever get that idea?!" and so on).

- **Don't laugh or make jokes about a student's question or viewpoint.** Many humorous questions are based on misperceptions or lack of information. *A serious question deserves a serious answer.* You might respond by saying: "A lot of people think that, but actually . . ."

- **If you are embarrassed, admit it!** Admit early on that you don't know all the answers and will follow-up on questions you can't answer; "That's a good question! I'd like to know myself. Suppose I find out and let you know tomorrow?"

- **If you can't answer or are uncomfortable answering a question, refer the student to someone who can.** "That's a good question; I wish I could answer but (give the reason). I'll help you find someone that can answer it."

- **Preserve the student's (and the class's) confidence.** While keeping personal information confidential is imperative, in certain instances, it may not be possible. Explain that you may have a legal responsibility to contact authorities and agencies (e.g., police, social services, campus security) if a situation warrants (e.g., rape, assault, stalking).

(Adapted from: Ponto, E. in Learning 87,
Springhouse Corporation, 1111 Bethlehem Pike, Springhouse, PA 19477.)

Another point to keep in mind is that all of us are individuals with varying backgrounds and experiences that shape our values, beliefs, and behaviors. Effective teaching about sexual decisions or otherwise occurs when students are respected and their individuality acknowledged. Becoming aware of our own beliefs and assumptions about sexuality can have an impact on our teaching effectiveness. According to research, the following assumptions can inhibit student participation and learning:

- **All students come from "traditional" nuclear families.** Demographic trends clearly indicate this is not true. Today, there are more single parent, divorced, blended, and stepparent families than ever before. Moreover, some students may have grown up in families with unmarried heterosexual or homosexual parents with adopted or foster children. Clarifying "family values" to understand sexual beliefs and behaviors cannot always be considered in traditional "mom and dad" terms.

- **All students are heterosexual.** While difficult to accurately measure, estimates suggest that ten percent of students are *not* heterosexual. Some students may be questioning their sexuality and struggling with a variety of issues. Promoting inclusive and non-biased language (e.g., "partner" or "significant other") in instruction is crucial for creating a non-threatening, trusting environment for sex education.

- **All students are sexually involved.** Many students are *not* sexually active and may need support for their decision. Presenting information in the third person as opposed to the second person ("you") will minimize judgmental perceptions and "preaching."

- **No students are sexually involved.** Denying that students are (and have been since whatever age) sexually active can also impact your effectiveness. Focusing on helping students clarify their values, improve decision-making skills, have healthy relationships, and seek resources is more important than determining students' sexual involvement status.

- **All students' sexual involvements are consensual.** Statistics indicate that many students from grade school to college age have been, or are being, forced to have sex. Not everyone chooses to be sexually active. This is particularly true in college populations where statistics indicate that 1 in 6 female students will be raped. Having referral information and resources available for your students, even if they don't ask for it, is necessary.

- **Students who are "sexually active" are having "intercourse."** Many people participate in behaviors other than traditional penile/vaginal intercourse. Even defining what constitutes "sex" and "intercourse" varies from person to person. For example, recent studies indicate that teens (and even adults) do not view oral sex as "sex" and may engage in it as a "safer" alternative to penile/vaginal/anal intercourse. The point is: There are a whole range of behaviors—not just intercourse—that comprise healthy sexual expression and development.

(Adapted from: Krueger, M.M. (1993). Everyone is an exception: Assumptions to avoid in the sex education classroom. *Family Life Educator,* Fall 1993.)

A suggestion for teaching the information on alcohol is to use peer leaders to present the material and lead the discussion. These guest speakers are generally very well received. This gives students role models to question and follow. If peer leaders are not available, you need to be prepared to openly and honestly answer questions about your own behavior or at least be prepared to deal with questions about your behavior related to alcohol. Instructors can capitalize on the media and lead discussions about reports of incidents, often deaths, related to high-risk drinking among college students.

Understand what is really happening on your campus regarding alcohol use, alcohol policy, who enforces policy, and how they do it. You should also be well prepared to answer questions about local ordinances related to underage drinking, public drunkenness, DUI, and other alcohol-related offences. We strongly recommend that you contact the Office of Alcohol and Drug Programs and the many people on campus who are engaged in prevention and education related to college student drinking. The professionals can give you current information on behavior and policy. They may also be able to provide helpful materials.

It is important for you or guest lecturers to avoid trying to impose values on others. Also, the journal entry topics for this chapter are extremely personal and private. Therefore, it may be inappropriate for you to collect and read students' writings or answers. Before making this chapter's assignments, always offer students a choice to submit or not to submit their work. You may want to consider omitting this chapter's journal from course grade requirements all together. A visual check (without reading) of students who completed entries may be adequate toward participation points versus grade points. This approach may give students permission to honestly and openly complete the journaling activity on their own.

Suggested Outline for Addressing Topics in Chapter 10

Step 1   Begin with a lecture launcher or icebreaker activity

Step 2   Employ a variety of classroom activities

     a. Use the PowerPoint presentation
     b. Expand on key lesson themes
     c. Involve students in a group activity
     d. Involve peer leaders
     e. Engage students in learning through case studies

Step 2   Review
   a. Address common questions and concerns about the topic
   b. Writing reflection

Expanded Lesson Plan

Step 1   Lecture Launchers and Icebreakers

Ask students to give their definition of stress. After collecting several, introduce students to the physiological and psychological changes that occur when a person is stressed. Giving them a holistic picture of stress and the stress response will give them a clearer picture of how important it is for them to manage their own stress.

Invite a guest speaker to your class who can show your students some common techniques of self-defense. Perhaps your campus offers free classes on this topic and you can invite someone from a student life office or a counseling center. Arming students with tools to help them combat campus crime empowers them. It also helps make the theoretical chapter material feel more real.

Step 2   Classroom activities

   a.   Use the PowerPoint presentations to complement your mini-lecture.

   b.   Key Teaching Themes

   ### ALCOHOL USE
   1. Ask students to volunteer with a partner. Assign each team one of the situations listed below and ask them to develop a short role-play:
      • Dealing with a drunken peer who needs assistance
      • Confronting a friend whose alcohol use has created problems for them or others
      • Talking to their parents about alcohol use and information
   2. Give the students 10–15 minutes to prepare. Then, ask them to present their role-play for the class.
   3. Allow the class to process after each role-play is presented. Try to leave time for questions as well.

   c.   Group Activities
   The objective of this activity is to give students more practice with relaxation techniques. This activity can be facilitated by the peer leader.

   Suggestions
   1. Prepare students the day before by asking them to wear comfortable clothing. This is especially important if you decide the exercise is best served by having them lie on the floor. Make sure you arrange for some cushions or mats if you do so.
   2. Read the following prompts to the class in a soothing voice to demonstrate how they can control anxieties by deliberately relaxing.

   Settle back and get comfortable. Take a few moments to allow yourself to listen to your thoughts and to your body. If your thoughts get in the way of relaxing, imagine a blackboard in your mind and visualize yourself writing down all of your thoughts on the blackboard. Now put those thoughts aside for a while and know that you will be able to retrieve them later.

Now that you are ready to relax, begin by closing your eyes. Allow your breathing to become a little slower and a little deeper. Let your mind drift back into a tranquil, safe place that you have been in before. Try to recall everything that you could see, hear, and feel back there. Let those pleasant memories wash away any tension or discomfort.

To help yourself relax even further, take a brief journey through your body, allowing all of your muscles to become as comfortable and as relaxed as possible.

Begin by focusing on your feet up to your ankles, wiggling your feet or toes to help them to relax, then allowing that growing wave of relaxation to continue up into the muscles of the calves. As muscles relax, they stretch out and allow more blood to flow into them; therefore they gradually feel warmer and heavier.

Continue the process into the muscles of the thighs; gradually your legs should feel more and more comfortable and relaxed.

Then concentrate on all of the muscles up and down your spine, and feel the relaxation moving into your abdomen; as you do so you might also feel a pleasant sense of warmth moving out to every part of your body. Next, focus on the muscles of the chest. Each time you exhale, your chest muscles will relax just a little more. Let the feeling flow up into the muscles of the shoulders, washing away any tightness or tension, allowing the shoulder muscles to become loose and limp. And now the relaxation can seep out into the muscles of the arms and hands as they become heavy, limp, and warm.

Now move on to the muscles of the neck—front, sides, and back—imagining that your neck muscles are as floppy as a handful of rubber bands. And now relax the muscles of the face, letting the jaw, cheeks, and sides of the face hang loose and limp.

Now relax the eyes and the nose, the forehead and the scalp. Let any wrinkles just melt away. Now, taking a long, slow, deep breath, cleanse yourself of any remaining tension.

You might want to hand out copies to your students and suggest that they tape the script and play it back when they are in need of relaxation.

d.   *Peer Leader Assistance*
See the exercise above.

e. *Case Studies*

RORY

Rory is a pre-med student. Both of her parents are physicians. Growing up, Rory never thought about being anything but a physician. She says she wants to be a physician but also feels a lot of pressure from her parents to be one. She is aware of how competitive it is to get into medical school, so she's very concerned about getting good grades. As midterms approach, Rory feels herself getting more and more stressed. She's having trouble sleeping, feels sick to her stomach, and has completely lost her appetite. She has also gotten into several arguments with her roommate lately. To avoid further conflict, Rory tries to spend as much time away from her room as possible, often studying at the library until closing and then moving into her dorm's lounge. She often doesn't get to bed until three or four in the morning, even though she has a Spanish class that meets every day at 9 A.M.

Discussion Questions

1. What are some mistakes Rory is making in terms of dealing with her stress?
2. How could Rory better manage her stress?
3. Should Rory discuss her anxiety with her parents? What should she say?

JAMES

James is on an academic scholarship that requires him to maintain a certain grade point average. He's had a rough semester and needs to do well on his finals in order to pull the grades that will keep him on scholarship. James is often tense regardless of exam schedules, but when he found out he would have three finals on the same day, he had a meltdown. First, he was angry that his schedule turned out this way, and he has complained bitterly about it to anyone who would listen. Then he got into an argument with his roommate, who was listening to music while James was trying to study. The night before his exams, James studied at the library all night. He skipped breakfast the next morning because he wanted get to the classroom early. The teacher passed out the test and James began to read it. He felt absolute panic. All the typing on the page was running together, his vision was blurred, and he couldn't remember anything. The longer he sat there, the worse it got. Finally, he decided to guess on the questions and get out of the room as fast as he could. He was so upset, he skipped his next two finals as well. He spent the rest of the day hiding out in his bed, wondering what he was going to do and how he was going to tell his mother he failed out of school.

Discussion Questions

1. Is there anything James could have done to handle this situation better?
2. What was the cause of tension between James and his roommate?
3. What are some test-taking strategies that would have helped him do better on the test?
4. Should James approach his teachers about what happened with his final exams? What would be the best way for him to do this?
5. If you were James's professor, how would you handle this situation?

Step 3   Review

a.   *Address Common Questions and Concerns of First-Year Students*

- *How can I deal with the pressures of college? Sometimes I feel like I am going to explode.*
  Answer: Students need to know that this is a perfectly normal reaction. They also need to know it's something they can control. Emphasize to them that time management, stress inoculation, and relaxation techniques can all help to reduce that "I am going to explode" feeling.

- *Where can I go for help with stress management?*
  Answer: You may want to invite someone from your campus's counseling center to come speak to your students about their stress management resources. It's also a good idea to discuss other options, such as yoga/meditation classes.

- *Will people think I am weak if I get help with stress management?*
  Answer: Some students may have a difficult time asking for help because to them it feels like admitting failure. They need to know that all college students feel overwhelmed and overstressed at certain times and that there is no shame in getting help.

- *How do you find time to do stress management?*
  Answer: This is a common problem not only for students. Impress upon your class how important it is for them to schedule "me" time, whether it's to work out, prepare a healthy meal, get eight solid hours of sleep, or meditate.

- *I think I may have a STI, but I'm not sure. What should I do?*
  Answer: It is important that students not ignore this thought or their health. If they think they have been exposed, they should go and see someone right away. Some options are community health centers, student health services, their doctor, or the local hospital. From there they can get guidance about what steps they need to take to help themselves both physically and emotionally.

- *I had sex last night but didn't mean to. What do I do now?*
  Answer: This is a potentially serious situation for many students. Sometimes sex happens in haste or ignorance and may leave a student emotionally scarred, exposed to STIs, or even pregnant. Encourage students to seek help right away from student health services, their doctor, community health services, and counseling centers. They should check out both their physical and emotional health.

- *I am really uncomfortable with hearing and talking about this stuff in class and with members of the opposite sex present. Do I have to share my personal experiences and thoughts about sex or alcohol with my classmates or the teacher?*
  Answer: Some students will not be comfortable sharing their thoughts, experiences, or even opinions in class. It is important that you respect this and insist on mutual respect in the classroom. You will find enough students who want to share. Let them do so without putting quieter students on the spot. Tell students it's okay to keep these matters private.

b.   *Writing Reflection*

- The topics for this chapter are extremely personal and private. Therefore, it may be inappropriate for you to collect students' writings or answers.

Test Questions

Multiple Choice

Choose ONE answer per question.

1. When you are experiencing stress, your body undergoes rapid _____ changes.
   a. physiological
   b. behavioral
   c. emotional
   d. all of the above

2. According to the text, a regular five-ounce cup of coffee contains _____ milligrams of caffeine.
   a. 10–25
   b. 95–150
   c. 65–115
   d. none of the above

3. The best starting point for handling stress is to pay attention to
   a. diet and exercise.
   b. sleep and social activities.
   c. a and b
   d. none of the above

4. The National Sleep Foundation recommends that adults get _____ hours of sleep per night.
   a. 5
   b. 6
   c. 8
   d. 10

5. According to the text, the body usually gets rid of alcohol at the rate of
   a. one drink per hour.
   b. two drinks per hour.
   c. three drinks per hour.
   d. none of the above

6. In addition to abstinence, which of the following contraceptive methods offers protection from STIs when used correctly and consistently?
   a. Cervical cap
   b. Condom
   c. Diaphragm
   d. none of the above

True/False

7. STIs are only spread through genital contact.

8. You should aim for eight hours of sleep each night.

9. Caffeine consumption can impact your stress level.

10. Frequent heavy drinking can lead to an increased tolerance for alcohol and potentially alcoholism.

Short Answer

11. Describe three things that happen in your body or mind during the stress response.

12. List three ways to inoculate stress.

13. What are four techniques for managing stress?

14. Which contraceptive methods protect against HIV and STIs?

Essay

15. Discuss the relaxation techniques described in the text. What are they, and how do they work? How do these techniques help the body deal with stress?

16. Both men and women may feel pressures to become sexually active or to increase their sexual activity. Explain two "encouragers" and two "discouragers" that may impact someone's decision to have sex. In your answer, be sure you clearly identify which is which, and show how each contributes to a person's decision-making process.

17. Recently, college presidents have identified alcohol use as the number-one public health issue facing college students. Identify several guidelines that you follow to protect yourself from experiencing an alcohol-related problem and being the victim of someone else's alcohol-related behavior.

18. What do you believe is the greatest single threat to your health, safety, and academic performance? Why?

Answer Key

1. d, p. 114
2. c, p. 114
3. a, p. 114
4. c, p. 115
5. a, p. 118
6. b, p. 117
7. false, pp. 116–117
8. true, p. 115
9. true p. 114
10. true, p. 119

Web Resources

Personal Safety Tips   www.elon.edu/safety/protect/safetips.htm
From Elon University comes this great resource that helps arm students to protect themselves from campus crime.

Birth Control   www.plannedparenthood.org/bc/
This resource on birth control options is offered by Planned Parenthood, the world's largest and most trusted voluntary reproductive health care organization. It contains information about everything from abstinence to Depo-Provera ("the shot").

STI Online   sti.bmjjournals.com/
Sexually Transmitted Infections is the world's longest running international journal dealing with issues of sexual health and medicine. Each issue includes editorials, review articles, research methodology, clinico-pathological conferences, and correspondence.

Binge Drinking Epidemic   www.health.org/govpubs/prevalert/v5/2.aspx
From the Substance Abuse and Mental Health Services Administration Center for Substance Abuse Prevention comes this "Prevention Alert" about the growing problem of binge drinking on college campuses.

Facts about College Smoking   www.uri.edu/smokefree/facts.html
The University of Rhode Island hosts this page, which lists some startling facts about college-aged students and smoking.

For More Information

Benson, H. and Klipper, M. Z. (1976). *The relaxation response.* New York: HarperTorch.

Elkin, A. (1999). *Stress management for dummies.* New York: For Dummies.

Gaddes, P. (2000). *Dangerous dating: Helping young women say no to abusive relationships.* New York: Shaw Books.

Gowen, L. K. (2003). *Making sexual decisions: The ultimate teen guide.* Lanham, MD: Rowman and Littlefield.

Handsfield, H. H. (2000). *Color atlas and synopsis of sexually transmitted diseases.* New York: McGraw-Hill.

Trechsel, J. G. and Yee, R. (2002). *A morning cup of yoga: One simple, balanced routine for a lifetime of health and wellness.* Birmingham, AL: Crane Hill Publishers.

Wells, D. K. and Morris, B. C. (2000). *Keep safe!: 101 ways to enhance your safety and protect your family.* Eugene, OR: Harvest House.

Whitman, N. A., et al. (2000). *Student stress: Effects and solutions.* San Francisco: Jossey-Bass.

11

Experiencing College Life to the Fullest

Getting Involved on Campus and in the Wider Community

Chapter Objectives

1. To determine how to find a job if students must work during college
2. To explore the advantages and disadvantages of working during college
3. To discuss why working on campus is preferable to taking a job off-campus
4. To discover how being active in campus organizations can benefit students
5. To discuss what to know about joining campus groups
6. To explore what internships and co-op programs are and how they can benefit students
7. To recognize how students can embrace and work in support of campus diversity
8. To discover how to use service learning to clarify values, develop skills, and participate in activities to improve the community, region, and country

Timing of Chapter Coverage

The subject matter of this chapter is such that you can teach it at any time during the semester.

About This Chapter

A key to using this chapter successfully is to recognize that two-thirds of a college student's life is spent outside the classroom and what goes on during this time constitutes a vital part of the education students will receive and remember from their college years.

Statistically, residence hall living and involvement with campus organizations significantly increase the odds of academic survival and persistence. Many students will be commuters, but for those in residence halls, successful adjustment needs to be encouraged, and all students should make significant connection to at least one campus organization.

We are powerfully persuaded of the value of co-op programs and service learning for today's students. Trends in the area of service learning are particularly exciting, and you would be on sound empirical as well as philosophical ground to urge or require your students to participate in service learning. It is important for students to see service learning not only as something to do for others, but also something that will be of great value to themselves.

We offer several simple suggestions for dealing with this chapter: Use former freshmen — outstanding upperclassmen — to convey the importance of "Experiencing College Life to the Fullest" by showing your students how they have connected to the campus and the wider community. If your university offers a "Clubs and Organizations Fair," schedule this topic to coincide with that event. This is a perfect time to schedule visits to selected offices such as Service Learning, Study Abroad, Career and Job Centers and so on, or, invite speakers from the campus and community to speak to the class.

Suggested Outline for Addressing Topics in Chapter 11

Step 1   Begin with a lecture launcher or icebreaker activity

Step 2   Employ a variety of classroom activities

    a. Use the PowerPoint presentation
    b. Expand on key lesson themes
    c. Involve students in a group activity
    d. Involve peer leaders
    e. Engage students in learning through case studies

Step 3   Review

    a. Address common questions and concerns about the topic
    b. Writing reflection

Expanded Lesson Plan

Step 1   Lecture Launchers and Icebreakers

- Ask students to complete *How do You Measure Up* on page 125. Generate a discussion based on their responses and use this as a springboard to segue into the lecture.

Step 2   Classroom Activities

a.   Use the PowerPoint presentations to complement your mini-lecture.

b.   Key Teaching Themes

GET INVOLVED

Address points in the section on "Being Active in Campus and Community Life". Use the exercise at the top of page 127, Finding Your Niche, to generate questions from the students.

STUDY ABROAD/ SERVICE LEARNING/CO-OP CENTER VISITS

To make students aware of campus resources and how they can use them, either invite a representative from these offices to speak to the class or plan a class trip to these offices. Consider having the job placement office look at some students' résumés, possibly critiquing them in the classroom setting (you can have the office remove the students' names and addresses from the tops of the resumes to protect the students' privacy). Ask these representatives to distribute literature about their centers. This is a good way to demonstrate the commitment of your campus to the students' ultimate success. At the close of this unit your students will have identified, articulated, and started to integrate their interests, current skills, aptitudes, personality characteristics, and values.

EMBRACING CAMPUS DIVERSITY

For an unusual exercise in cultural diversity, I suggest using one from Dr. Chante Cox of the Carnegie Mellon University Psychology Department regarding her list of well-known and little-known negative stereotypes that African-Americans have about white Americans. Go over the list with your class. Everyone knows the negative stereotypes about African-Americans that white Americans sometimes have, but most white students have never heard the ones about themselves. In fact, they are often surprised to hear that there are any! As they hear what they are, they are typically puzzled and astonished. After a while, all they can do is laugh out loud: These stereotypes are not merely untrue; they are ridiculous. And that is precisely the point: *All* stereotypes are ridiculous. This exercise tends to come in under the student's radar, so to speak. It is not like the usual cultural diversity lessons they have had and may have grown tired of, and it tends to work well. It really does encourage students to seek greater diversity in their relationships.

c. *Group Activities*
- Have students jot down five campus organizations they find interesting. Collect responses and form small "interest groups" of students who listed similar things. Have each group identify what kinds of careers their interests might be useful for. Another activity would be to form four-member teams who share the same academic major or similar career interests. One pair of students within each team might research internship opportunities while the other pair investigates related service learning opportunities. The group's final product would represent a composite of available "experiential learning" opportunities tied to their majors, interests, or skills.

d. *Peer Leader Assistance*
- In addition to actively participating in the activities surrounding this topic, peer leaders should make sure that props and logical arrangements for these activities are scheduled ahead of time.

e. *Case Studies*

PROFESSOR JONES, HEATHER, AND SUE

Professor Jones had the students in his first-year seminar write journals every week. This week two young women's journals caused him some concern. Both women were eighteen years old and attending college for the first time. Neither was a very good student, but neither was failing either. Heather seemed happy, cheerful, and energetic. She didn't make many contributions in class, but she was always present and loved talking to her fellow students before and after each class. Sue was much quieter. She sometimes missed class, but she was very apologetic when she did. In contrast to Heather's good cheer, Sue often had a certain look of sadness on her face, and she was much less outgoing with her classmates than Heather was. Sue usually did, however, manage to read her assignments and try to make some contributions to the class although her confidence seemed a little shaky. Here are the journal entries that caused Professor Jones to be concerned: Heather wrote, "I told him that I wanted to go out with him tonight, so he came and picked me up. We went and hung out at the fraternity house where I met all his friends; it was fun. It was soo wild! I saw more drugs, drinking, and fighting in one night than I have in three months. Every guy there was a complete scammer." A few days later, she wrote, "Tonight was soo much fun! All my friends came to the house to watch my brother's band play. We danced and drank and had a good time. It was completely wild! There were drug deals being made every time I turned around and people doing pot in the room I was in. There were a bunch of drunken jerks fighting about nothing and some guy cutting his wrists in front of everyone. Things like this just don't happen at home!"

Here is what Sue wrote in her journal: "I'm sitting in my dorm room by myself, thinking too much, as usual. I really need to be studying, but I just can't concentrate on school. It's weird how you don't think about something very often and then all of a sudden it hits you and then it's all you can think about. I miss my dad! It's been about nine years since he died and I can't believe how much of my life he's missed. The little girl I was when he died is barely the same woman I am now. Each day it gets harder to remember the way he looked in person or the way his voice sounded. I used to love to hear him laugh and now I can't even recall what his laugh sounded like. Maybe I'm thinking about him tonight because we had a parents' cookout this weekend. I loved having my mom and my stepdad there, but I would have given anything to have had my dad there. It's like he's half of me, and none of my friends will ever see where that half originated. I never got a chance to really know about him like I now know about my mom. You know as you get older, your parents start to share more about their past with you, and you can laugh and relate with them. But I didn't have that with my dad. Sometimes I do or say something and wonder if I got that from him. I hate nights like this. I miss him so much it literally hurts. When will I see him again? Will I ever see him again? The pain is unbearable."

Discussion Questions

1. Do you think professor Jones should be worried about Heather and Sue?
2. Do you think either of them has a serious problem? If so, what is it?
3. What should professor Jones say to Heather and to Sue?
4. How could their parents approach them in a positive and helpful way?
5. If Heather and Sue were your roommates, what would you do or say? What can and should Heather and Sue do for themselves?
6. Would their situations be different if they joined a club or organization?
7. How do you think Heather and Sue probably fared in college and in their lives after they graduated, or do you think they probably would not make it through college?

Step 3   Review

a.   *Address Common Questions and Concerns of First-Year Students*
   •   *Why do professors think their dumb courses are the only things in our lives? Relationships and social activities are obviously more important to us, not to mention the jobs we have to work to pay the bills.*

       Answer: While student journals suggest that relationships take center stage with students, they must learn to balance college and work with their personal lives. Reminding them of their career and educational goals will help to reinforce this. Students need to be careful not to allow outside activities interfere with coursework and studying. Help them to learn how to find balance.

   •   *I'm afraid I'll say something that will offend someone of another race.*

       Answer: It will happen, and sometimes you may not even know it. Use common sense and work on building a relationship with someone you like. Don't go out of your way to be friendly with other minority students if you really have little in common with them. Ask yourself, "Would I be friends with this person if he or she were from the same culture as I am?"

   •   *I don't think I'm part of any cultural group.*

       Answer: Everyone is part of some cultural group. It might be interesting to ask members of your family where your ancestors came from. You may discover that rather than being part of one group exclusively, you are actually a mixture of several.

b.   *Writing Reflection*
   •   Have students complete the Portfolio exercise at the end of the chapter.

Test Questions

Multiple Choice

Choose ONE answer per question.

1. Fraternities and sororities can provide
    a. a link to a social network.   c. support.
    b. camaraderie.   d. all of the above

2. In simple terms, in co-op programs you spend some time on campus and the rest
    a. at home.   c. in temporary jobs in your field.
    b. at another university.   d. none of the above

3. Through an internship you will learn about
    a. the nature of the industry.   c. a and b.
    b. the daily work routine.   d. none of the above

4. Hate crimes include
    a. physical assault.   c. intimidation.
    b. vandalism.   d. all of the above

5. Service learning does not involve
    a. serving.   c. learning.
    b. linking.   d. rivalry.

6. Value dualisms are
    a. only formed in childhood.
    b. easily recognized.
    c. consistent across cultures.
    d. conflicts within a set of beliefs.

True/False

7. Working to register new voters is not a form of civic engagement.

8. There are even fraternities and sororities for specific racial or ethnic groups.

9. Service learning is the same thing as community service.

10. Becoming involved on or off-campus helps you gain valuable knowledge.

Short Answer

11. Give two examples of a special-interest group.

12. Give two examples of value dualisms.

13. List four avenues for locating off-campus work.

Essay

14. Describe the three components of service learning.

15. Research a club or organization you are interested in joining. What is attracting you to this organization? How will your affiliation with that organization benefit you, and what can you contribute to the organization?

Answer Key

1. d, p. 127	6. d, p. 132
2. c, p. 129	7. false, p. 133
3. c, p. 129	8. true, p. 127
4. d, p. 131	9. false, p. 132
5. d, p. 132	10. true, p. 127

Web Resources

CollegeValues.org   www.collegevalues.org/

CollegeValues.org is a Web site for the *Journal of College and Character and the Character Clearinghouse* published by the Center for the Study of College Student Values at Florida State University. It focuses on character development in college as well as how colleges and universities influence—both intentionally and unintentionally—the moral and civic learning and behaviors of college students.

Ethics and International Affairs   www.cceia.org/

The Carnegie Council on Ethics and International Affairs is an independent, non-profit organization. It offers programs and publications that provoke thinking and dialogue about the urgent and complex ethical dilemmas involved in international decision making.

Personal Responsibility   www.heritage.org/Research/PoliticalPhilosophy/HL515.cfm

You can find this lecture on "The American Tradition of Personal Responsibility" on the Web site for The Heritage Foundation, a conservative organization. The essay, while pushing a specific agenda, raises several questions for your students to think about while learning the material from this chapter.

National Service-Learning Clearinghouse   www.servicelearning.org/

This is the homepage of the Learn and Serve America National Service-Learning Clearinghouse (NSLC), which supports the service-learning community in higher education, kindergarten through grade twelve, community-based initiatives and tribal programs, as well as all others interested in strengthening schools and communities using service-learning techniques and methodologies.

Campus Compact   www.compact.org

Campus Compact is a national membership organization of college and university presidents committed to helping students develop the values and skills of citizenship through participating in public and community service.

Relationships   www.literacynet.org/lp/learn2learn/students/relationships.html

For students interested in knowing more about how their learning styles affect their relationships, this site offers bulleted lists of qualities common among types as well as strengths and challenges for each individual.

For More Information

Bringle, R. G., et al. (2003). *The measure of service learning: Research scales to assess student experiences.* Washington, D.C.: American Psychological Association.

Gray, J. (1993). *Men are from Mars, women are from Venus: A practical guide for improving communication and getting what you want in your relationships.* New York: HarperCollins.

Josephson, M. S. and Hanson, W., eds. (1998). *The power of character: Prominent Americans talk about life, family, work, values, and more.* San Francisco: Jossey-Bass.

Kaye, C. B. (2003). *The complete guide to service learning: Proven, practical ways to engage students in civic responsibility, academic curriculum, and social action.* Minneapolis: Free Spirit Press.

Miller, J. G. (1999). *Personal accountability: Powerful and practical ideas for you and your organization.* Denver: Denver Press.

Smith, B. L. and McCann, J. eds. (2001). *Reinventing ourselves: Interdisciplinary education, collaborative learning, and experimentation in higher education.* Bolton, MA: Anker Pub. Co.

12 Making the Right Choices for Your Major and Career

Planning Early and Keeping an Open Mind

Chapter Objectives

1. To illustrate how changes in the workplace that have occurred in students' lifetime will affect how they will prepare for a career

2. To introduce what personal qualities and skills are essential for career success in the information age

3. To discuss what personal factors affect career choices

4. To discuss how students can explore their personal interests as a path to identifying potential career choices

5. To learn how students can build a winning résumé and write a persuasive cover letter

6. To discuss what to do to prepare for a job interview

7. To explore what programs and activities are available for getting on-the-job experience and helping students land a job in their chosen careers

Timing of Chapter Coverage

The introduction of career decision-making material could be addressed immediately following Chapter 3 or in the middle of the term. By then, students have had time to adjust to their new environments and are getting acclimated to college classes and exams. Working through this chapter will allow students to sort out their interests and reaffirm their educational pursuits. This does not mean that they have to declare a major or have a specific career in mind when the course is over. However, they should have a better sense of who they are and what classes may be of interest to them.

About This Chapter

Goal setting in general, and career planning in particular, are real problem areas for students, especially first-year students. Probably only a few of your students are self-disciplined enough to engage in rigorous career planning. Others are simply not mentally ready to undertake career planning. Still others, especially older students, are so sure of the choices they've already made that they will regard any time you spend on career planning as a waste of their time.

Therefore, at best you can expect your students to understand the process of career planning by the end of this chapter. They should know the major steps of the process, how to perform them, and what resources exist on your campus to help them as they move along the path of goal setting and career planning. This seemingly "modest" achievement is really very important in that it lets the students know that there is a process they can follow, and it informs them of who can help them when they are ready. It is also another way of demonstrating your concern for them.

Before beginning this section, you should decide how much time you want to devote to it. Assess where your students' attitudes and motivation for career planning lie and then decide on how much and what you will cover from this chapter. Use some of the Lecture Launchers or chapter exercises to stimulate interest before you teach the chapter. Depending on your students' attitudes toward career planning, you might decide to spend time on other activities.

Suggested Outline for Addressing Topics in Chapter 12

Step 1   Begin with a lecture launcher or icebreaker activity

Step 2   Employ a variety of classroom activities

a. Use the PowerPoint presentation
b. Expand on key lesson themes
c. Involve students in a group activity
d. Involve peer leaders
e. Engage students in learning through case studies

Step 3   Review

a. Address common questions and concerns about the topic
b. Writing reflection

Expanded Lesson Plan

Step 1   Lecture Launchers and Icebreakers

- Today's students cannot only choose their careers, but they will be able to change their careers later in life if they so desire. Encourage students to think about members of their families and the attitudes they have toward their work. Try to end the discussion by having them recognize that they have choices. After this discussion, ask your students to submit at least two questions about career choices. Specifically, what do they want to learn from the chapter? You might then compile these questions in a list and distribute them to the whole class to be used as a guide to the chapter. These questions will also be a guide to you as you teach the unit.

- Depending on your class, it may be of value to share some of your career development experiences. Think back to your first year in college. Did you begin college knowing what career you wanted? If so, did you stick to that decision? Were you uncomfortable with that inevitable question, "What's your major?" Did you think that you were alone in feeling clueless about your future? Encourage your students to share their career goals (or lack of goals) with each other. This will help them realize that many of their fellow students are as undecided as they are. You want to let them know that being undecided is okay. Teaching career planning is also a way of letting first-year students know that there are sources that can help them make decisions.

Step 2   Classroom Activities

a.   *Use the PowerPoint presentations to complement your mini-lecture.*

b.   *Key Teaching Themes*

THE INFORMATION ECONOMY

Address points in the section on Careers in the Information Economy. Use this to help students begin a conversation on their career interests.

CHOOSING CAREERS

Choosing courses and careers is something that an academic advisor may assist students with. However, there are other sources of information that students can use to make these important decisions. Place students in small groups to generate ideas for alternate sources of information that will be of use to them as they choose courses and faculty. Such sources of information might include the college catalog or bulletin; departmental course descriptions; course syllabi (obtained from other students, academic department offices, or directly from faculty); required textbooks (can be viewed at the college bookstore); faculty members (other than official academic advisors); and other students' recommendations. After you've discussed the Holland Career Inventory, students can share with their groups how they can connect their interests and majors to careers.

CAREER COUNSELOR/CENTER VISIT

To make students aware of campus resources and how they can use them, either invite your campus career counselor to class or plan a class trip to the counseling center. In either case, the career counselor can provide an authoritative summary of what you have already taught. Consider having the career counselor look at some students' résumés, possibly critiquing them in the classroom setting (you can have the counselor remove the students' names and addresses from the tops of the résumés to protect the students' privacy). Ask the counselor to distribute literature about the counseling center and all of the resources available to your students.

c.   *Group Activities*
*   Have teams of students generate a list of academic or personal problems they might need help with. Arrange the problems into categories and identify campus resources that can offer help.
*   Have students jot down five things they find interesting. Collect responses and form small "interest groups" of students who listed similar things. Have each group identify what kinds of careers their interests might be useful for. Students could also form four-member teams with the same academic major or similar career interests. One pair of students within each team might research internship opportunities while the other pair investigates related service learning opportunities. The group's final product would represent a composite of available "experiential learning" opportunities tied to their majors, interests, and skills.

d.   *Peer Leader Assistance*
*   Consider inviting a recent graduate of your institution into the classroom to discuss his or her experiences in searching for a major and related career. This could be a graduate who had trouble choosing a major or who has had more than one career. You could also arrange for a small panel of several seniors who can discuss how they went about making their decisions about courses and careers.

e. *Case Studies*

ANDREW

For as long as he could remember, Andrew had wanted to be a physician. So when he entered college, he majored in science as preparation for medical school. But although he earned good grades in his science courses, he found that he was bored with science in general. He made an appointment with his adviser and told him how he felt. His advisor said, "Andrew, I know what you mean. Lots of people go through this stage. But your grades are so good that I'm going to urge you to continue. Then, when you begin medical school, you can decide whether or not you want to stay there. If you don't, your education will have prepared you for a number of other careers, so what have you got to lose?" Andrew left the office feeling confused. "If I don't enjoy something," he said, "why should I keep on doing it?"

Discussion Questions

1. What's your opinion of the advice the advisor gave Andrew?
2. Physicians make good money. Is this a strong reason for Andrew to stick to his plans? Explain your answer.
3. How might a visit to the career center provide Andrew with some insight into his dilemma?
4. Andrew is getting a solid liberal arts education anyway. What's he really got to lose by staying on track for the present?

BECCA

Becca came to college and took classes for a year and a half. Not knowing what she wanted to major in, she didn't do that well in her classes. So, she decided to take a year off from college and work. Becca has been working as a bookkeeper for a printing company for one semester now. While she likes making money, she is still not satisfied and thinks that going back to college may be a good idea for her. However, she still has no clue of what career or major to choose. Becca is apprehensive about going back to college because she is so undecided.

Discussion Questions

1. What is Becca's dilemma?
2. What suggestions could you give Becca?
3. What issues should Becca address before deciding whether or not to go back to school?
4. How can Becca come to a decision about college and work?
5. Where can Becca go for help?

Step 3   Review

a.   *Address Common Questions and Concerns of First-Year Students*

- *I'm only a first-year student. Why should I be concerned with careers now?*
  Answer: Many students will not see the need for exploring majors or careers so early in their education. Explain to them that selecting a major and career is a process that involves self-knowledge and takes time. Encourage them to begin this process right away so that when the time comes for a decision, they will be prepared.

- *If it's true that my generation will change careers five times, why is career planning so important?*
  Answer: It is true that the workplace has changed dramatically for employees and that nowadays people make multiple career changes. Emphasize to students that the decisions they make in college will impact where they end up in the workplace. Encourage them to find different ways to use their majors for employment and to undertake a thorough career-planning program.

- *I already know what I want to do. Why do I have to go through all this boring stuff?*
  Answer: While some students will have a strong sense of their career, today's work world is constantly changing and will require that they come well prepared and with the understanding that there are no guarantees of ongoing employment. They stand to change jobs more than ever. Explain to students that they must explore and identify their interests, values, goals, personality type, and aptitudes and accurately link them to possible careers.

- *How do I know I will have the skills and competencies I need when I graduate?*
  Answer: The responsibility for knowing what skills are needed for various professions falls on the student. The last thing they want to do is graduate from college and find out that they are missing a skill, competency, or certification that is critical for employment in a particular field. Emphasize that we are all responsible for our careers. Students can do research to find out what skills and competencies are needed for the fields they have chosen.

b.   *Writing Reflection*

- Have students complete the Portfolio exercise on page 147.

Test Questions

Multiple Choice

Choose ONE answer per question.

1. As a result of workforce restructuring wrought by the Information Economy, major changes have taken place in
   a. how we work.
   c. the ways we prepare students for the world of work.
   b. where we work.
   d. all of the above

2. To advance your career, you must
   a. accept the risks that accompany employment.
   b. plan for the future.
   c. a and b
   d. none of the above

3. According to John Holland, for someone in the _____ category, accounting would be an ideal occupation.
   a. realistic
   c. investigative
   b. social
   d. conventional

4. According to John Holland, for someone in the _____ category, marine science would be an ideal occupation.
   a. realistic
   c. investigative
   b. social
   d. conventional

5. When writing a résumé, you should
   a. aim for it to be one page in length.
   b. place your hobbies and interests at the top to make yourself appear more well-rounded.
   c. list a minimum of five personal and professional references.
   d. print it out on bright paper to distinguish you from the other applicants.

6. The process of making a career choice begins with
   a. understanding your values and motivations.
   b. identifying your interests.
   c. a and b
   d. none of the above

True/False

7. A college degree does not guarantee employment.

8. A commitment to lifelong learning will help keep you employable.

9. You are, more or less, solely responsible for your career.

Short Answer

10. Name the six general categories of people identified by John Holland.

11. List at least three factors affecting career choice.

12. List four ways you can look at yourself in regard to making a career choice

Essay

13. How does the text define the economy of the early twenty-first century? As you are preparing to begin your career, what are some things you need to keep in mind to "survive the changing economy?"

14. Which of Holland's six categories do you best fall into? What are some careers that Holland predicts would appeal to you? Which one do you find yourself most interested in? How would you go about investigating the career?

15. If you have already identified a career that you wish to pursue, shadow someone for a day who is presently working in that field. Write an essay describing your activities for the day, why you wish to pursue this field, what strengths you presently possess that support your desire to pursue this field, and what you still need to do to in order to qualify for a position in this field.

Answer Key

1. d, p. 138
2. c, p. 141
3. d, pp. 142–143
4. c, pp. 142–143
5. a, p. 144

6. c, p 140
7. true, p. 141
8. true, p. 141
9. true, p. 141

Web Resources

Choosing a Major   **www2.ucsc.edu/porter/choosing.html**
This page debunks some of the myths about choosing a major such as "Picking a major and a career are basically the same thing" and "The major I pick now will determine my lifelong career."

The Career Key   **www.careerkey.org/english/**
Direct your students to The Career Key, a free test that measures skills, abilities, values, interest, and personality. It also offers information about the jobs for which it identifies aptitude.

Résumés   **jobsmart.org/tools/resume/index.cfm.**
A feature of JobStar Central, this page offers information about creating a résumé as well as samples of different résumé formats. It includes a feature that can help students determine what kind of résumé would work best for them.

Cover Letters   **www.careerlab.com/letters/default.htm.**
From CareerLab, this page offers great strategies for writing various types of cover letters—everything from answering a want ad to sending the most appropriate thank-you letter after an interview. Each article is accompanied by an extensive set of examples your students can use as models.

Career Planning   **quintcareers.com/** and **careerbuilder.com**
This site is a career planning and job-hunting resource guide. **Careerbuilder.com** is a comprehensive career-planning Web site.

The Self-Directed Search   **www.self-directed-search.com/**
For a nominal fee, your students can take the official John Holland Self-Directed Search assessment on this page. The test takes 15 minutes and results include a list of occupations, fields of study, and even leisure activities well-suited to the taker's particular type.

What Can I Do with a Major In . . . ?   **www.uncwil.edu/stuaff/career/Majors/**
The University of North Carolina at Wilmington offers this site, which will give your students an idea of what career paths their major will open up for them.

For More Information

Block, J. A., et al. (1997). *101 best resumes: Endorsed by the professional association of resume writers.* New York: McGraw-Hill Trade.

Gordon, V. N., et al. (2000). *Academic advising: A comprehensive handbook.* San Francisco: Jossey-Bass.

Lore, N. (1998). *The pathfinder: How to choose or change your career for a lifetime of satisfaction and success.* New York: Fireside.

MacHado, J., ed. (2002). *Fishing for a major.* New York: Natavi Guides, Inc.

Prince, J. P. and Heiser, L. J. (2000). *Essentials of career interest assessment.* San Francisco: John Wiley and Sons.